PERFECT PHRASES™

for

NEW EMPLOYEE ORIENTATION AND ONBOARDING

PERFECT PHRASES™

for

NEW EMPLOYEE ORIENTATION AND ONBOARDING

**Hundreds of ready-to-use phrases
to train and retain your top talent**

Brenda Hampel and Erika Lamont

New York   Chicago   San Francisco   Lisbon   London   Madrid   Mexico City
Milan   New Delhi   San Juan   Seoul   Singapore   Sydney   Toronto

The McGraw·Hill Companies

1 2 3 4 5 6 7 8 9 10 11 12 13 14 15 16 17   QFR/QFR   1 9 8 7 6 5 4 3 2 1

ISBN   978-0-07-176650-0
MHID   0-07-176650-2

Library of Congress Cataloging-in-Publication Data

Hampel, Brenda.
   Perfect phrases for new employee orientation and onboarding : hundreds of ready-to-use phrases to train and retain your top talent / by Brenda Hampel and Erika Lamont.
       p.   cm. -- (Perfect phrases series)
   ISBN 978-0-07-176650-0 (pbk.)
   1. Employee orientation.   2. Employees—Training of.   3. Business communication.   I. Lamont, Erika.   II. Title.

HF5549.5.I53H36   2011
658.3′1242014—dc22   2011008411

Contents

Preface

Buyer's remorse—consumers have it, and new employees have it. Have you ever started a new job and thought, "What did I get myself into?" or "Do they really want me here?" or "Did anyone know that today is my first day?" Unfortunately, many new employees are asking these questions and having these thoughts. The organizations that they have just joined did not take the time to prepare and "onboard" them properly. Statistics still report up to a 40 percent failure rate of new leaders and that the highest employee turnover rates occur within the first three years on the job.

Landing a new job or hiring a new employee is one of the few events in the workplace that give us a clean slate—a chance to start at the beginning and build. Unfortunately, many times neither the new employee nor the hiring manager takes advantage of this unique opportunity and both end up with buyer's remorse. The new employee is excited and highly engaged but looking for support, information, and tools to be able to get her job done and understand the organization. The manager is so relieved to have completed the selection process and filled the position that he forgets the employee is new and expects her to hit the ground running and start delivering results. The two are already on different paths, but unfortunately, these two paths lead to the same place—frustration, confusion, disillusionment, and ultimately, failure.

This is completely avoidable.

Our work with organizations, managers, and new hires is focused on helping each create a road map that keeps everyone focused on the right thing at the right time. A structured onboarding program keeps both new employees and hiring managers out of the "returns line." So, when we were offered the opportunity to work with McGraw-Hill on the orientation and onboarding title for its impactful and very successful *Perfect Phrases* series, we were thrilled!

As we talk with people in both operations and human resources roles at conferences and when we talk with colleagues and clients, they continue to tell us that onboarding is both a hot and evolving topic. This means that the term *onboarding* itself still has several definitions, and how onboarding is actually structured (or not!) and played out in organizations looks very different company to company. This *Perfect Phrases* book gives us the chance to share best practices and perfect phrases that further define onboarding, how it is different from orientation, and the positive impact successful onboarding can have on individuals and the organization. Our goal is to provide you with straightforward, practical tools and ideas that you can put to work regardless of the size or type of your organization.

So, the next time you accept a new role or hire a new employee, you will know what to do when and avoid that "What did I get myself into?" question.

Acknowledgments

We gratefully acknowledge the professional support of Anne Bruce, speaker, author, and coach, who has guided, mentored, and cheered us through this publishing journey. We value her as a colleague and as a friend.

Our editor at McGraw-Hill, Mary Therese Church, has been a source of encouragement and direction for this, our first book project. We thank her for her faith in us and for bringing us into the Perfect Phrases family!

We appreciate the trust and support of our clients, especially those who have entrusted their onboarding work with us: TJX Companies, Audi of America, Volkswagen Group of America, The Ohio State University Medical Center, WD Partners, Cardinal Health, Nationwide Children's Hospital, Chico's FAS, Greif Inc., and Tween Brands. It is because of your commitment to the work of your organizations and the passion that you bring that we can do what we do.

Finally, we are most thankful for the love and support of our husbands and families, Jeff, Alex, and Jordan Hampel; Michael, Elizabeth, and Maggie Lamont; Erika's parents, Francine and Max Buban; sister Anneliese Thomas; and for the many other family and friends who have encouraged and supported us through this adventure.

Introduction

How do you define onboarding? As we mentioned in the Preface, the definition and application of onboarding is still evolving. Therefore it is important for us to work from a common definition for the purposes of this book.

Onboarding is a structured process, lasting anywhere between three and six months, that positions an organization's new employees with the organization's vision, strategies, goals, and culture. It integrates the new employee into the organization, business unit or function, and role. Successful onboarding experiences are a partnership of the new employees, their managers, and human resources partners.

In other words, onboarding is all about alignment and getting the right people involved at the right time. Onboarding begins once the employee accepts his or her new position and typically goes through the first few months. The employee then transitions into the performance management and development stages of the talent management cycle. This cycle begins with the selection process, then onboarding, then performance management, leadership development, and succession planning, where it circles back to selection, which also includes internal promotions. Onboarding should be positioned as part of this larger strategic cycle for attracting, developing, and retaining talent in your organization.

Studies confirm that when a new employee accepts a position, his engagement level for that organization and job is at its highest level. An effective onboarding program builds on this high engagement and continues to reinforce the employee's decision to take the position. Highly engaged employees are more productive faster, and the organization sees a quicker return on its investment in those employees. The impact on the bottom line is real and clear! Organizations spend tens of millions of dollars on their recruiting and selection processes each year, so it only makes good business sense to invest some in making sure that those new hires "stick" and are able to grow with the company.

Perfect Phrases for New Employee Orientation and Onboarding is a powerful, quick reference guide for managers, HR professionals, and executive coaches who are actively engaged in helping their leaders and employees onboard, or transition, into their new roles and cultures. This book describes how to build a solid business case for creating an onboarding experience with Perfect Phrases to insert into presentations, e-mails, interviews, and conversations. It also provides a time-based road map for managers, HR partners, and new hires as they navigate their first few months together.

Our experience in onboarding is that the new hires, their managers, and human resources partners all make assumptions about what everyone needs to do (and not do) during those first critical days and months. We have built a successful business by consulting to people in all of these roles on how to effectively manage onboarding. Any new hire, manager, or human resources professional can make the strategies and Perfect

Phrases in this book work for himself or herself and his or her organization.

A Note About Questions

Some of the Perfect Phrases in this book are in the form of questions. We feel that questions can actually be the most powerful way to communicate. Questions allow you to gather information, create and understand context, influence the listener, create buy-in, and coach effectively. Using questions as a new employee is a great way to understand the culture without sounding arrogant or judgmental. It allows for more open dialogue that helps the employee gain key knowledge, build important relationships, and open the door for feedback, all of which are critical to the successful onboarding experience. These questions can also be used strategically by managers and HR partners to gather feedback about your new employees, your onboarding experience, or your process partners. Use them generously.

PERFECT PHRASES™

for

NEW EMPLOYEE ORIENTATION AND ONBOARDING

CHAPTER 1

The Difference Between Orientation and Onboarding and Why Organizations Can't Afford Not to Onboard

Since the mid-90s, onboarding has been "on the radar" of most HR managers inside larger organizations. Michael Watkins, with his book *The First 90 Days*, made onboarding a relevant business topic, and many organizations followed his lead to create onboarding experiences for their new hires. Unfortunately, however, these experiences varied greatly and had mixed results. Some organizations defined onboarding similarly to orientation, while others left it to the new hires themselves and provided little or no organizational support.

Onboarding plays an important role as a key program that should exist between the recruitment and selection process and performance management programs in an organization.

Onboarding is the bridge between the résumé screening, interviewing, and selection of a job candidate and the annual review measuring how that employee is doing in her job. Orientation, on the other hand, is the event that usually takes place on or near day one and provides an information dump of the organization and a plethora of paperwork to complete.

Perfect Phrases for Defining Orientation

Use these phrases in an internal presentation or e-mail to explain how orientation is different from onboarding:

→ New employee orientation is an event.

→ Orientation is more a one-way flow of information to the new employee.

→ Orientation is a one-size-fits-all program with most or all positions expected to attend.

→ The audience of new employee orientation is typically externally hired associates of all levels, but typically the new leaders do not participate.

→ Orientation is usually owned and led by the human resources function.

→ Orientation focuses on the logistical and the tactical.

→ It is typically classroom-style learning.

→ Orientation provides a one-way exposure and view to the organization's culture.

→ Employees are still new after orientation.

→ Orientation can be used effectively to introduce the onboarding program.

Perfect Phrases for Defining Onboarding

Use these phrases in an internal presentation or e-mail to explain how onboarding is different from orientation:

➜ Onboarding is a process that begins upon acceptance of the job and typically lasts through the first 90 to 180 days.

➜ Onboarding allows information to flow through several different channels from the organization to the new employee and from the new employee to the organization.

➜ Onboarding delivers organizational overview information to a diverse group of new employees with consistency, yet with context to the particular employee's situation.

➜ The onboarding experience is customized by a new employee's role in a particular function or department of the organization.

➜ Onboarding reflects best practices when it is facilitated by Human Resources in close partnership with the hiring manager and the new employee's ownership and active engagement.

➜ Onboarding is integrative and strategic.

➜ Onboarding delivers functional and role-specific information to the individual employee in a just-in-time model.

➜ Onboarding uses a blended learning approach.

➜ Onboarding's success results when the organization allows the new employees to observe and participate in the culture; it gives the new employees feedback and then helps them make adjustments based on that feedback.

→ It allows a "live and learn" experience to the new employees to enable them to understand the culture of the organization.

→ Onboarding is important for both newly hired and newly promoted employees.

→ Employees are fully integrated and not new after the onboarding experience.

Perfect Phrases for Building the Business Case for Onboarding

In most organizations, new business processes are not automatically approved, funded, and readily accepted as part of how things are done. Creating the "so what?" or the business case for such a new program is the critical first step. There are many reasons to create an onboarding program in your organization. The trick is finding the reasons that are the most relevant and have the most clout with the decision makers.

These phrases can be used by your onboarding project team to create questionnaires and interviews as they gather data to support the building of a program:

→ What is important in your business and your culture?

→ Is it all about the numbers?

→ Do key people need to be "presold" on an idea?

→ Does Human Resources have the influence to initiate this type of program?

→ Should the case for onboarding be made by some other part of the organization?

→ Do you need both quantitative and qualitative data to present your case?

→ It is important to have senior leadership sponsorship.

→ Where's the "pain"?

→ What are the onboarding "horror stories"?

→ What business issues will an onboarding program solve?

→ Are you experiencing heavy turnover in the first one to three years?

→ Are your hiring managers frustrated because their new employees are not productive quickly?

→ Are your new employees making mistakes that are costing your organization more resources than is acceptable?

→ What do new employees say about their experiences?

→ What do hiring managers need from their new hires in the first year?

→ What do your leaders see as the burning issues around new talent?

→ What do current or tenured employees say about the new employee experience?

→ Identify the things that are done now in orientation and onboarding that are working.

→ Integrate what is currently working into your orientation and onboarding processes.

→ Identify an onboarding champion in your organization and engage him or her.

Perfect Phrases for Defining Onboarding Objectives

Defining onboarding objectives is by far the most important step in building your onboarding business case. Clearly stating what you want to achieve with your onboarding program will not only help in selling the concept to the rest of the organization, but it will keep you on track as you create the action items, the roles and responsibilities, and the measurement (or metrics) of the process.

These phrases serve as a guide for the onboarding project team leader, or onboarding champion, as she helps the team or the organization build the foundation for the onboarding program:

→ Get clear about what business issues onboarding will address.

→ What are the organization's objectives, and how can the onboarding objectives support them?

→ Build measurement tools and metrics to reflect the onboarding program's objectives.

→ Who is/are our audience(s)?

- → Is the audience all employees, new leaders, internal promotions, external hires, merger and acquisition employees, contractors, and/or temporaries?

- → Increase our speed to performance of new hires by _____%.

- → Reduce early turnover (for example, in the first three years) by _____%.

- → Increase the engagement levels of our new employees.

- → Align our new employees with our culture.

- → Preserve our culture as we grow.

- → Reduce the time for new employees to meet their first-year objectives.

- → Increase the sales volumes of new employees by _____%.

- → Get new managers ready for their increased roles.

- → Reduce turnover of new managers by _____%.

- → Prevent "culture shock" for our new employees.

- → Maintain the core components of our culture as we grow.

- → Leverage our onboarding program to attract and retain top talent.

- → Use our onboarding experience to strengthen our employment brand.

- → Create a seamless transition from the recruitment and selection process to the onboarding program so the new employees continue to be highly engaged and their decision to join the organization is reinforced.

→ Create a presentation that tells the story of how the onboarding objectives support the business case. (For a sample template of a Building the Business Case Power-Point presentation, go to www.connectthedotsconsulting .com and choose "Onboarding.")

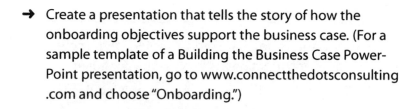

Perfect Phrases for Defining Roles and Responsibilities

A good onboarding program lays out the specific roles and responsibilities of all the participants. We find that the best-practice onboarding programs use the "three-legged stool" model of onboarding. The hiring manager, the HR partner, and the new employee are all key participants in the process and have specific roles that are played out in their action items. If any one of them fails to perform his or her part of the process, one of the legs is "broken" and that onboarding experience is not as effective as it could be. We also find it extremely helpful to spell out the roles and responsibilities of each of these process part-ners and provide these guidelines to participants in all of these roles as they are being introduced to the onboarding program. They can refer to the guidelines throughout the experience to keep each other on track.

Use these phrases to create your Onboarding Process Partner Roles and Responsibility Summary to communicate this impor-tant part of the onboarding process.

The HR Partner

→ Serves as the onboarding process guide for the new employee and functions as a guide and confidant.

→ Facilitates the establishment of onboarding objectives, "early wins," and the stakeholder analysis.

→ Shares key documents and related insights with the new employee.

→ Focuses on creating role clarity throughout the new employee's onboarding process.

→ Facilitates the team alignment process (for new managers).

→ Formally and informally gathers feedback regarding the new employee's effectiveness and assists in identifying and implementing solutions and developmental actions.

The Hiring Manager

→ Serves as the primary information source regarding the role expectations and direction of the new employee.

→ Acts as the sounding board for the new employee and provides feedback and direction as the new employee learns about his or her role and the organization.

→ Shares insight and advice about the employee's team and key stakeholders.

→ Collaborates with the HR partner to ensure alignment of his or her actions throughout the new employee's onboarding process.

■ The New Employee

→ Takes the initiative to work with his or her hiring manager to set and understand onboarding objectives, identify targeted onboarding meetings, and facilitate other transitioning activities.

→ Reaches out to process partners when assistance is needed and is receptive to feedback and direction from those partners.

→ Maintains a willingness to develop and demonstrate a deep understanding of and respect for the organization, its people, and its practices.

Defining roles and responsibilities, outlining and articulating your onboarding program's objectives, building the business case for onboarding, and defining orientation and onboarding are all important components of your foundational work.

CHAPTER 2

Perfect Phrases for the Three Secrets to Onboarding Success: Knowledge, Relationships, and Feedback

In our years of working with all types of organizations and individuals, we have been able to identify and articulate the three most important components of a successful onboarding program. Each time we work with a client organization to build or customize its program and coach individuals, we focus the roles, resources, and delivery around three main themes:

- Knowledge
- Relationships
- Feedback

The first theme, knowledge, refers to the information that the new employees need to acquire throughout their onboarding.

It starts with a broad overview of organizational vision, mission, values, and history and then builds to current strategies, processes, and culture. From there, new associates need timely knowledge about their function, their teams, and their roles.

The next theme, building relationships, is critically important to a new hire's success. This component is especially important for employees who are brought into an organization to bring about change or lead through a crisis or turnaround. But it is, of course, vital to any new employee's success as he executes his objectives with and through others.

Lastly, the providing of timely and actionable feedback is usually the missing link in most onboarding programs. Organizations are typically not set up to give formal feedback, and the informal feedback on which they rely can be incomplete or missing entirely. Impressions and perceptions about the new employees are formed very early, so it is important to incorporate both quantitative and qualitative early feedback into the onboarding program, usually at the 45- to 60-day mark.

These three components are the foundation on which you build your onboarding program that allows you to see results that are consistent with your objectives.

Perfect Phrases for Organization-Level or Company Objectives

Creating an onboarding plan with emphasis on gaining knowledge, building relationships, and getting feedback is critical to a new employee's success. Use the following phrases to create onboarding objectives that support gaining knowledge about the organization, the business unit or function of that new hire, and his or her role.

These objectives give new employees key pieces of information that they need as a foundation to build upon. Achieving organization-level objectives provides new employees with context as they have more interactions and experiences and build their knowledge base.

→ If the new employee is from a different industry, it is critical to start with "Business 101" objectives to get him or her up to speed with the basics.

→ If the new employee is from the same industry, it is important to start with how your organization is different from its competitors.

→ Study and build an understanding of the strategic vision and direction of (organization).

→ Gain an understanding of the overall structure of the organization.

→ Learn the organization's core competencies.

→ Develop an understanding of what are the important components of our culture.

➜ Develop an understanding of the organizational core values.

➜ Understand the leadership success factors or leadership competencies.

➜ Understand how (product/service) is (produced, created, bought) and how it is processed and delivered to the customer.

➜ Develop an understanding of the organization's core processes.

➜ Learn and be able to articulate what makes us unique in the marketplace.

➜ Develop a base knowledge of the business, what makes us unique, and how we're able to offer consistent value to our customer every day.

➜ Develop an understanding of what is consistent in every business and what is unique.

➜ Build relationships with key stakeholders.

➜ Become familiar with the organization's terms, acronyms, and language.

➜ Develop an understanding of our business model.

> ➜ Get a working knowledge of our financials.

> ➜ Learn the decision-making process.

> ➜ Understand the meeting cadence.

➜ Develop an understanding of the distinctiveness and brand positioning of the organization.

Perfect Phrases for Division-Level Objectives

The next level on which the new hire needs to focus is the division or business unit. Many of the objectives are the same as the organization-level objectives; however, they are focused on the division instead of the overall organization. The new employee will likely focus on both organization and division-level objectives at the same time. It is important to be purposeful when identifying the timing for each objective so they build on one another.

→ Learn about the division's overall structure.

→ Build an understanding of how each division fits into the organization.

→ Determine how all the functions within the organization operate within a division.

→ Learn how each division drives the overall business.

→ Develop an understanding of the corporate and divisional structures; understand who the key stakeholders are and your role in partnering with them.

→ Develop an understanding of the important components of the divisional culture.

→ Schedule trips with (these designated key stakeholders).

→ Build an understanding of the overall division strategy.

→ Become familiar with the division financials.

→ Understand the competitive landscape for the division and how it is different from the organization's.

→ Gain an understanding of how the division measures performance.

→ Develop an understanding of divisional terminology and language.

→ Build key relationships with key people within the division.

→ Develop a detailed understanding of the role of my function in the division.

→ Become familiar with the division's decision-making processes.

→ Create strategies for effectively dealing with division stakeholders.

Perfect Phrases for Department-Level Objectives

The next level of objectives on which new employees need to focus is departmental. Many times hiring managers make the mistake of only focusing on this level, driven by the "hit-the-ground-running" mentality. However, the new employee needs the perspective and context of both the organizational and divisional objectives.

→ Understand how the department is structured.

→ Build an understanding of who the formal and informal leaders in the department are.

→ Determine how key decisions are made.

→ Develop an understanding of how to present new ideas.

→ Gain an understanding of the key weekly, monthly, and quarterly meeting cadence.

→ Become aware of important daily, weekly, and monthly deadlines.

→ Understand the key reports that are used in the department on a regular basis.

→ Develop an understanding of the unique culture of the department.

Perfect Phrases for Objectives for Other Departments

In addition to achieving objectives focused on the new employee's department, she also needs to build knowledge about other departments, especially those with which the new hire will work closely. Typically this list of objectives will be shorter and more targeted.

Here is a list of functions for which the new hire may need learning objectives:

- Marketing
- Finance
- Information technology
- Distribution
- Sales
- Customer service
- Human resources
- Administration

Examples of objectives for these areas for non-marketing, non-finance, or non–information technology associates, etc., are listed here.

→ Understand previous year and most recent quarter financial results.

→ Understand close calendar and pre-close calendar.

→ Understand travel and expense policy.

→ Understand accounts payable cutoff and time frames.

→ Understand chart of accounts for coding invoices.

→ Understand sales flow (i.e., come in through POS, etc.).

→ Gain understanding of various departments and areas within Finance.

→ Understand payroll process, paid time off submission process, etc.

Perfect Phrases for Role-Level Objectives

Now it is time to focus on the new hire's role. What does she need to learn about her new role? As she learns about her job, the new hire is building a solid foundation of knowledge about the organization, division, and department. This approach to learning makes the new hire a well-rounded and highly engaged employee.

→ Get clarity about the role and why it exists.

→ Gain an understanding of the manager's expectations of the role.

→ Build knowledge about the history of the role.

→ Understand who the key peers in the department and outside of the department are.

→ Develop a clear understanding of how success will be measured.

→ Understand the charter for this role.

→ Build an understanding of the recruitment process that took place—were there any internal candidates to be aware of?

→ Determine how the role functions within the department, business unit, and organization.

→ What expectations does the organization have about this role?

→ Is this a newly created or existing position?

→ How long has the position been open?

→ Go slow to go fast.

Perfect Phrases for Building Relationships

As the saying goes, "It's not *what* you know, but *who* you know." This really applies to the new hire after the job is landed. But it's up to the organization to help the new hire figure out who those people are. It's great to let some relationships develop on their own, but in order for the new hire and the organization to get the most impact out of these relationships, they must be targeted as ones that support the new person's actual deliverables.

How do you identify who these individuals are? The best place to start is with the hiring manager, regardless of whether the new hire has been with the company and has accepted a new role internally or she has been hired from the outside. The hiring manager typically has the best view to the purpose of the role and the deliverables expected and needed. The following Perfect Phrases help the hiring manager identify the new hire's key stakeholders with whom she needs to build relationships to be successful.

Perfect Phrases for the Hiring Manager in Identifying Key Stakeholders

→ Describe the position.

→ Outline the key deliverables of the role.

→ Is the job newly created, or is it an existing job?

→ Tell me the peers or other team members from whom the new hire will have to get information on a regular basis.

→ Why was this person chosen for the job?

→ Identify the areas of the business in which the new hire lacks experience.

→ Outline the key deliverables for the role for the next 30, 60, and 90 days.

→ Which people can help the new employee achieve these deliverables?

→ Think through the "quick wins" that will be important for the new hire to achieve.

→ Identify the three to five people with whom the new hire needs to build relationships.

→ Who are the best individuals to help the new hire understand the culture?

→ Based on the new hire's role, outline any individuals outside of the organization such as customers, vendors, or community members the new hire needs to build relationships with.

Perfect Phrases for Meet-and-Greet Meetings

Most organizations plan for new hires to have a series of meet-and-greet meetings. The intent is to introduce the new hire to peers and other coworkers so they can get to know one another. However, most of these meetings lack direction and purpose. In fact, many of the meetings get cancelled or rescheduled several times. This leaves the new hires frustrated and left to figure many things out for themselves.

In order to purposefully facilitate new hires building key relationships, the next step is to communicate to the current employees their responsibilities in supporting the onboarding of new hires and to provide structure for the meet-and-greet meetings.

→ Discuss the new employee's background.

→ Share your background both at (company name) and any previous experience.

→ Provide an overview of your role and team.

→ Discuss how your team and the new employee's team interact.

→ Share your thoughts on how effectively the team currently works together.

→ Ask the new employee how he or she is experiencing the culture.

→ Make suggestions on other coworkers the new hire may want to connect with.

→ Invite the new hire to attend a company event.

→ Give the new hire perspective about the culture.

→ Identify specific follow-up items.

→ Agree to any next steps.

Perfect Phrases for New Hires Meeting Stakeholders

Now that the stage has been properly set, the new employee is ready to build relationships with key stakeholders who will support her success. These Perfect Phrases are for the new hire to use when meeting with key stakeholders such as his or her team, peers, HR partner, manager, internal customers, or any other key stakeholder in the organization.

Of course, peers are a key group of individuals with whom new hires need to build relationships. The following Perfect Phrases give new hires conversation topics that build both relationships and knowledge.

→ Let's have coffee (lunch, breakfast, dinner).

→ I would like to talk with you more about _____
_____.

→ I would appreciate your insight on _____
  _____.

→ I would appreciate your take on _____
  _____.

→ I am interested in hearing more about your ideas for _____
  _____.

→ I'm interested in understanding more about your professional background.

→ Tell me about your role here.

→ What do you like about it?

→ How would you describe our department?

→ Describe how our organization works.

→ How would you describe the leadership style of my manager?

→ What does a typical week, month, or quarter look like for you (your department or function)?

→ When you talk about where you work to those outside of the organization, what do you say?

→ What are some of the barriers that you have?

→ What motivates you?

→ What are the top three current priorities for your department?

→ How do you see my role aligning with the business?

→ How does my role support and partner with your department?

→ What can be improved in the way these departments work together?

→ How can we best partner together?

→ What would be the best way to provide ongoing information to you about your department?

→ Is there anyone else in your area with whom I should speak?

→ Which business in the company represents the "best in class"?

→ I would like/need your input on _____.

→ What do you wish you had known when you were new here?

→ What advice do you have for me?

→ How do you measure success?

→ How does the organization measure success?

→ What is best way to communicate with you?

→ Is there something that needs to be addressed immediately that I can do for you?

→ What are your thoughts on _____?

→ Do you see a need to change _____? Why or why not?

→ What are the things that "keep you up at night"?

→ Who are the strong performers on your team, and what makes them that way?

Perfect Phrases for Giving Constructive Onboarding Feedback

No news is not good news during the first few days, weeks, and months on the job! Feedback, in other words, "how am I doing?" is probably the single most helpful thing that a new hire can get from her new organization. Unfortunately, most people are not that skilled at giving feedback at all, much less giving constructive feedback that can be vital to a new employee's success.

The manager, a peer, a direct report, or an HR partner can use these phrases to give the new employee specific, constructive feedback that will allow him to understand what he needs to adjust to be more successful in the organization. (Chapter 10 has more Perfect Phrases for giving feedback.)

→ I would like to give you some feedback about your first few days (weeks).

→ Would you like some initial feedback?

→ I have some thoughts on how you are fitting in. Do you have a few minutes to talk about it with me?

→ Would you like to talk more about what you heard in that meeting?

→ The way you handled _____ was great. Keep it up!

→ You are really tuned in about _____.

→ Another way you can use your experience is _____ _____.

→ The team has noticed _____ and really appreciates it.

→ I noticed that in your presentation you _____
_____.
Let me explain why that doesn't really fit in our culture.

→ The culture here is tricky. Let's talk about how you are being perceived.

→ Your team has noticed a couple of behaviors that may continue to get in your way. Let me explain how, and we can talk through some strategies to address them.

→ It's really important in our organization that you always
_____.

→ It's really important in our organization that you never
_____.

→ I noticed a couple of things in that last meeting that I need to make you aware of.

→ Although you may not be comfortable with _____, let me explain why it's important in our organization.

→ Our leadership team looks for _____, and it would be important to show this early.

→ Sometimes feedback is tough, but it's important to know how you are being perceived. I have some information that will really help your onboarding be successful.

Perfect Phrases from Key Stakeholders That Indicate Onboarding "Red Flags"

Here are some Perfect Phrases from others that indicate the new employee may be derailing and will need support to get back on track.

→ The jury is still out about the new hire.

→ Did you see how the hire handled that issue? She doesn't seem to understand how we manage customer issues.

→ The new hire is working hard to fit in.

→ I'm not sure she is a good fit.

→ The new hire mentions his previous company in almost every conversation. That needs to stop.

→ The new hire needs to do more listening.

→ New hires need to ask a lot of questions, but this one makes more statements.

→ I am concerned about whether or not the new hire understands our business model.

→ Who interviewed the new hire?

→ It seems like the new hire has been here long enough to understand our key products.

→ It doesn't seem like the new hire is connecting to his team members.

→ Our new team member doesn't go to lunch with the rest of the group.

Building knowledge, forming relationships with the right people, and getting actionable feedback about how the new hires are transitioning are the three key components of a successful onboarding process. Focus on these elements and the onboarding process and experience will be targeted, purposeful, and position the new associate for long-term success.

CHAPTER 3

Perfect Phrases for the Prestart Phase of Onboarding

Think back to the last time that you accepted a new job—either internally or moving to a new company. How did you feel about the job, your new manager, and the company? Research has shown that new employees are highly engaged and feel very positive about all three. That level of engagement is tough to beat. However, organizations and hiring managers have much more influence than they typically use after an offer has been accepted. So much energy has been put into the recruitment process that once it is completed, the hiring manager and HR partner usually move very quickly to the "productivity cycle." They want that new hire to "hit the ground running." The manager thinks, "We hired a smart person, and I am sure that she will have an immediate impact."

If the productivity cycle kicks in too soon, the new hire is set up to fall short of expectations. The new employee is anxious to learn more about her role, department, and company, so meet her where she is and leverage the prestart time period, which is the time between when the job has been accepted and day one.

Perfect Phrases the Hiring Manager Can Use with the New Hire in Phone Conversations or E-Mail Messages

→ Welcome!

→ We are lucky to have you!

→ So glad you're here!

→ We are really happy to have you on our team.

→ What questions do you have so far?

→ We will work together to put together a plan for your first few months.

→ Let's stay connected. What's the best way for you? (e-mail, phone, text, etc.).

→ Your first day is _____, and you will want to be here at _____.

→ Orientation is held _____ at _____, and after it we will _____.

→ The first few weeks can be overwhelming, so let's walk through what will be going on.

→ Let's talk through any questions you might have.

Perfect Phrases for the Prestart Phase of Onboarding

The HR partner can use these phrases with the new hire in phone conversations or e-mail messages:

→ I will help you and your manager build a plan to help you with your first 90 days.

→ Here at (organization) we have an onboarding experience that will help you be successful.

→ Let's talk about what to expect your first week.

→ Let me tell you about our orientation.

→ We have a formal orientation, and here's what to expect.

→ Our orientation is pretty informal, and here is what it will be like.

→ Let's review some logistics like where to park, what to wear, and when to be here on your first day.

→ We will send you some materials to tell you more about our organization.

→ You can log onto (website) to read more about our company.

→ Our business hours are _____.

→ What questions do you have so far?

→ Your hiring manager (or a peer) will also be contacting you before your first day.

→ I understand that it can be difficult to say that you are leaving to (previous employer), so what are your concerns?

Perfect Phrases if the New Employee Is Relocating

HR partners or hiring managers can use these for new associates who will be relocating for their new roles. Special attention needs to be paid to those associates who will be moving.

→ We understand that your (family, significant other) will be going through a transition too.

→ Let's talk about what you will need for your relocation.

→ A relocation specialist will be contacting you, and please don't hesitate to call me with any questions.

→ Moving is stressful—let me know how we can help.

→ How is your (significant other) adjusting to your move?

→ Is there anything we can do to make the transition smoother?

→ Based on what you told me earlier, here are some resources that your family might be interested in. (Add links or brochures for shopping, schools, churches, or leisure activities in the community.)

→ Here is where you can find information about our community activities. (Insert.)

→ I need to fill you in on a couple of things that are happening here now.

→ Things happen quickly around here, and we don't want you to be out of the loop.

→ There have been a few changes since we last spoke. Let me fill you in.

→ Here is a copy of the announcement that went out about you joining the company. Do you have any questions?

By taking advantage of the prestart phase, hiring managers and HR partners set the stage for a purposeful onboarding plan, as well as a positive and engaging experience for the new hire.

CHAPTER 4

Week 1: Perfect Phrases for Getting Off to a Great Start

Another common onboarding mistake that organizations make is not to be purposeful about the first week for a new employee. It is important to think about the details of what it means to be new in your organization. Remember the new hire doesn't know the routine, where things are located, and what the current priorities are. Make sure to include the simple and obvious so that nothing is forgotten or taken for granted. New employees may ask questions, but there are many things they don't even know to ask. Be proactive and anticipate their questions and needs. What impression do you want to make on day one? What experience do you want the new hire to have? Use these Perfect Phrases to help you answer these questions and to position you to be purposeful about this critical time period.

Perfect Phrases to Define the New Hire's Experience

→ Link to the employment brand.

→ Connect to the recruitment materials and conversations immediately.

→ Define and include some type of orientation, either formal or informal.

Perfect Phrases to Outline the Logistical Parts of Week 1

→ Set up the new employee's work area.

→ Connect the phone and establish a phone number.

→ Create the new hire's e-mail address and set it up in the system.

→ Set up the new hire's system log-in and any other appropriate access required for the job.

→ Place basic supplies in the new hire's work area.

→ Make sure that the new hire has proper access to the building or facilities on day one.

→ Order business cards, a nameplate, and a company credit card if applicable.

→ Clearly communicate both internally and with the hire who will greet her and take her to orientation, as well as who will escort her from orientation to the work area.

→ The first week agenda should always include:

  → A tour of the building, facility, or campus

  → An organizational overview (a big org chart)

  → Lunch partners for each day

  → A work area orientation

  → Introductions to the immediate working team

→ The first week should *not* include:

  → The new hire sitting alone for hours reading manuals and binders or e-learning

  → Overscheduling of meetings, tours, etc.

  → Attending any meetings without context

  → The new hire's manager being out of town (without a plan)

Perfect Phrases for the Rest of Week 1

Often the first day is easy to plan and fill with orientation, paper-work, system training, etc. What is the plan for days two through five? Again, be purposeful!

→ Focus on learning, building on the information shared in recruitment, prestart, and orientation.

→ Go slow to go fast.

→ Create a week one calendar for the new hire.

→ Allow time for the new hire to:

  → Set up her office

  → Read orientation and training materials

  → Explore the company intranet and other systems

→ Schedule lunch with coworkers and other key stakeholders.

→ Prepare the new employee for meetings and interactions, explaining what is expected of her:

  → Listen and learn.

  → Ask questions.

  → Give input and make suggestions.

  → Share best practices for previous work experiences.

→ Schedule time, formal or informal, to debrief the new hire's experiences.

Perfect Phrases for Week 1 Check-In

The manager or HR partner may use these Perfect Phrases to get a sense of how the first week is going and if there are any initial concerns or "red flags" in the onboarding experience.

→ Tell me about your first day.

→ What things have surprised you?

→ What questions do you have?

→ Who have you met?

Perfect Phrases for Logistics Check-In

Remember that you do not get "extra points" for getting the logistics right for your new employees. However, if you do not get them right, the new hire wonders if the organization was ready for him. In addition, the new hire has to spend time trying to figure out how to get his office set up, get onto the system, etc.

→ Let's check out your work space.

    → Is your computer set up?

    → What about your phone and voice mail?

    → Were you able to access your e-mail and our intranet?

    → Let us know what additional supplies you need.

→ Your work space was set up with the basics. If you need additional items, check with _____.

→ Do you have everything you need for your office?

→ IT/phone/security support questions can be answered by _____.

→ The way to get office supplies is _____.

Perfect Phrases for Debriefing Orientation

Do you remember what was covered when you went through orientation? You probably do not remember very much. It is difficult for new hires to absorb and retain the information and details covered in the hour-plus of most orientation programs. It is important for the hiring manager to spend time reviewing the information that was covered and how it relates to the new hire's department and role.

→ Let's talk about orientation. What did you learn?

→ What questions do you have about orientation?

→ Let's review the organizational structure and how our department fits in.

→ I would like to talk through our executive level and where our leader fits into the structure.

→ Our values are an important part of our culture. Let's talk about how you will see them in action.

→ There is a lot of information "thrown" at you during orientation; let's review the key learning points.

Perfect Phrases for Week 1 Debrief

The following phrases allow the hiring manager to both understand how the new hire's first week went and begin to focus on continued learning and the onboarding plan.

→ It's really important to have onboarding objectives, and I have drafted a list to help you get started.

→ "Early wins" are quick hits that will help you gain traction in your new role.

→ Ask lots of questions and actively listen as you learn.

→ Some advice that I wish I had been given when I started here is _____.

→ The people in your department who can answer questions about how things work around here are _____
_____.

→ Let's set up a regular time to talk.

→ Let's take a tour of the building (campus).

→ I'll take you to see the departments that you will be working with most often.

→ Let me introduce you to the people you'll be working with first.

→ Let's have lunch.

→ Have you met _____?

→ Have you met your team (coworkers, clients, peers)?

→ How is your family doing with your move?

→ Some community resources that you might be interested in are _____.

→ We have great (schools, churches, parks, etc.), and here is a link for more information.

→ On Fridays, the dress code is casual and jeans are OK.

→ When I started here, the thing that surprised me most was

_____.

→ It's best to listen and ask questions to get more information before making suggestions.

→ When you attend the _____ meeting, make sure that you _____.

→ The function (department, area) that has the most power in our organization is_____.

→ What questions do you have?

→ Your onboarding plan will lay out specific objectives in a time frame that will keep your first months on track.

→ Some of the great perks we have here are (café, dry cleaning, banking, special discounts, etc.).

→ We also have (on-site daycare, a workout facility, oil changing, errand service, etc.) that you can use as an employee here.

→ If you would like to get involved, we have groups who (run, bike, volunteer, host a book club, etc.).

→ Philanthropy and volunteer opportunities offered at our organization are _____.

You only have one chance for a good and positive first impression. Week 1 sets the tone for the new employee's onboarding experience. By purposefully creating a welcoming experience that lets the new hire know that he was expected and the organization was ready for him, his decision to join the organization will be reinforced. This is the first step in keeping your new employees highly engaged.

CHAPTER 5

Month 1: Perfect Phrases for the Honeymoon

Some new employees get a longer honeymoon than others do, so it is important to stay focused on the onboarding plan during the first 30 days. Often in larger, more mature organizations, employees stay "new" for three to four months or sometimes longer. We know of one large organization that considers employees new until they have celebrated their two-year anniversary! On the other extreme are smaller, high-growth organizations that are hiring employees weekly or even daily. In this environment, an employee is probably only "new" until the next person comes in behind him. In any case, there should be time built into the schedules for one-on-one meetings with the manager and HR partner, if possible.

Staying in touch with your new employees is the key to surfacing and addressing onboarding issues before they get too serious. Conversations, e-mails, and other types of check-ins are the best way to know whether a new hire is floundering or flourishing.

Perfect Phrases That Say "I'm Still on My Honeymoon"

→ Everyone here has been really nice and helpful.

→ My manager has been great!

→ I really like the energy of this place.

→ This is fun, and I get paid for it too!

→ People are happy here.

→ My coworkers have really helped me fit in.

→ There are a lot of smart people here.

→ I have a good understanding of what I am supposed to do.

→ My onboarding plan has helped me stay focused.

→ HR has met with me a couple of times to see how things are going.

→ I got good feedback on the first report that I turned in.

→ I like how everyone seems to work together.

→ The communication flow is open and honest.

→ The leaders here seem really engaged.

→ I love all the perks of this company!

→ My friends are jealous that I get to work here.

→ I tell my (significant other, family) how lucky I am to work here!

→ People have told me that I am "getting it."

→ People have said they forget that I am "new."

Perfect Phrases That Say "The Honeymoon's Over!"

→ It's been a bad week (month).

→ I thought I had this place figured out.

→ Wow! This place is a lot different than I thought.

→ People told me that (organization) was _____, but I didn't believe them until now.

→ At my old company, we _____.

→ This is not what I signed up for.

→ My manager keeps changing her mind, and I am confused.

→ I thought I was responsible for _____.

→ I think I might be in over my head.

→ Can I do this?

→ It's been harder than I thought it would be to _____ _____.

→ I am not sure that I'm making any progress.

→ I got some feedback that I don't understand.

→ Nobody gets what I am trying to do.

→ I thought I was supposed to _____.

→ Why is it taking so long to _____?

→ I am frustrated.

→ I am angry.

→ I talked with a recruiter.

→ My former boss called me and wants to have lunch.

→ My friends from (former company) are calling me and trying to talk me into coming back.

Perfect Phrases to Coach New Employees Through the First 30 Days

The first month of a new job is a whirlwind of activities and emotions for new employees, so it is important to stay close to them so you know when that honeymoon period is still in full swing, when it starts to wane, and when it is completely over. Remember to touch on a wide variety of onboarding issues for new employees: for example, logistics (office/work space setup), relocation, personal transition, the onboarding plan, role clarity, and the employee's relationship with the hiring manager. The key is to catch things and address them before they get too big and start to erode the employee's engagement in her job and with the organization.

There will be a fair amount of repetition in the types of questions you ask and the topics you cover over the course of the onboarding period, and this is purposeful. As the employee gets more familiar with the organization and his role, he will see things differently, so the answers to the same questions will change. After two or three months, things look different than they did after the first month. The HR partner and hiring manager will be able to measure the employee's level of engagement and onboarding success based on this information.

→ Do you have everything you need for your office?

→ Are there any other logistical (compensation, benefits, relocation, etc.) issues that are outstanding that I can help you with or get someone to help you with?

→ Are you able to meet with/get time with the people we identified in your onboarding plan?

→ How are the conversations (with these key stakeholders) going?

→ I am sure that you feel a little overwhelmed right now. Let's have a conversation about what you should be focusing on.

→ Let's talk about your onboarding plan and make sure that all of your questions are answered.

→ If your role is not what you expected it to be, then let's discuss the differences between your expectations and what you are experiencing now.

→ A good first step in resolving an issue about your role is to talk with your manager about how she defines the role and then how you are experiencing it.

→ We have several people in the department (function, organization, etc.) who can help you. Here is how you contact them and some suggestions for how to best use their support.

→ I understand that you are still getting things settled at home and with your family. Moving to a new city can be stressful—how is it going?

→ I understand how you miss your former organization (or community from which the employee relocated). What's different here? Is there anything that has pleasantly surprised you? Or not?

Perfect Phrases to Coach Learning and Doing

One of the biggest frustrations for new employees in their first month is that they don't feel like they are actually doing anything. They read, they observe, and they attend meetings, which are all things that are critical to this early phase of the onboarding process. However, both the employee and the organization can get impatient for results. This is particularly true of new leaders and experienced hires that have been brought in to make changes or to implement their knowledge into the organization. One way to address this is as simple as adding one word to your vocabulary—*because*. This is a powerful word when talking with new employees about their onboarding activities. The idea is to connect the activities to particular outcomes, results, and objectives that mean something for the role and the organization. This allows the manager or HR partner to coach the new employee to learn and do.

→ You are going to this meeting because _____
   _____.

→ I would like you to work on this project because _____
   _____.

→ I recommend that you review this process because _____
_____.

→ Your relationship with _____ is very important
because _____.

→ When you visit _____, make sure you look for
_____ because _____
_____.

→ It's important that you do this research because _____
_____.

→ You might want to take some more time with that
because _____.

→ _____ is a key person in our organization because
_____.

→ We have found this works best because _____
_____.

→ This training will be critical for you because _____
_____.

→ Measuring the results and understanding their impact is
part of our core processes because _____
_____.

Remember that the first month on the job and in a new culture can be fast, fun, but a bit overwhelming. New employees
also may feel like they are not really "doing" anything yet, so it is
important to stay close to them and understand what they are
thinking and feeling.

CHAPTER 6

Months 2 and 3: The Onboarding Plan Continued and the Wrong Fit

Most organizations, and most new employees for that matter, only have the tolerance for about three or four months of a formal onboarding program. After this time, the new associates may still be learning, but they don't want to be called out as "new" anymore. However, because this time is short and intense, it is critical that the onboarding plan is created, implemented, and leveraged to its fullest potential. There is the danger of losing focus and energy around onboarding at the 60- or 70-day mark. This is when the hiring manager, HR partner, or new employee himself or herself needs to step up and take an active role in getting the plan in progress again to avoid any kind of derailment or, worse yet, failure.

Both the manager and the HR partner will want to meet at least monthly with the new employee to review progress on the onboarding plan. It is always a good idea to have both ask similar questions and then talk to each other to make sure that they are getting consistent information from the new employee. That way they can make sure that there are no gaps or miscommunications. Redundancy is a good thing in onboarding.

Perfect Phrases for Keeping the Onboarding Plan on Track

The manager or HR partner can use these Perfect Phrases to make sure that the onboarding plan is staying on track through months 2 and 3:

→ Let's walk through your onboarding plan, starting with the objectives we outlined for the first month. What progress have you made?

→ Are there additional resources that you need in order to meet your onboarding objectives?

→ What is different about your role than you expected?

→ What has pleasantly surprised you about our culture?

→ What things have been barriers for you in your first few weeks here?

→ Tell me about the status of your key stakeholder (personal network or meet-and-greet meetings). Have these appointments been kept, and have the participants been engaged? Who else do you need to participate?

→ Let's talk about any onboarding challenges that you might have now and how I can support you.

→ Are there any outstanding logistical issues that you need to resolve?

→ What about your personal transition? Does your (spouse, significant other, children) need any additional resources that we can supply?

→ What feedback have you gathered so far, and what have you done with it?

→ Here is the feedback that I have been hearing: _____
_____.

→ Let's talk about the organizational (functional or depart-mental) meetings that you have participated in and how they are connected to your onboarding objectives.

→ What concerns do you have about meeting your onboard-ing objectives?

Perfect Phrases to Discuss the Onboarding Progress of a New Employee

The hiring manager and the HR partner should plan to check in with each other periodically throughout the onboarding process as well. They can share information and observations about the new employee and identify those areas in which they can help reinforce key ideas and themes. They can also share feedback that they have heard about how the new employee is fitting into the culture, and the HR partner can address any disconnects between the new employee and the hiring manager.

Use these Perfect Phrases for meetings between the manager and the HR partner to discuss the onboarding progress of the new employee:

→ How do you think _____ is doing?

→ Has he met your initial expectations?

→ Have you seen him demonstrate the knowledge, skills, or abilities that you believed were there in the selection process?

→ This is my perspective: _____.

→ The feedback I have gotten on her is _____.

→ Have you seen any evidence of derailing or disconnecting behaviors? If so, have you shared that feedback with the new employee? How did she respond?

→ How do you think that she is adapting to our culture, and what examples can you share?

→ What do you know about the status of the new employee's key stakeholder meetings?

→ Do you have any concerns about the new employee's ability to be successful here? Why or why not?

→ What specific onboarding challenges is the new employee experiencing?

→ Have you worked through any of these challenges with him?

→ How can I support you in assisting with those challenges?

→ Your new employee has shared a couple of concerns with me about her onboarding plan. Let me give you some examples, and we can talk about how best to approach this.

→ What other needs or activities have you identified that could help the new employee in his onboarding?

Perfect Phrases That Indicate the New Hire May Be a Poor Fit

There are times when either the hiring manager, HR partner, or new hire realizes that things are not going well—the new hire is "not a good fit." The regular discussions, feedback mechanisms, and structured interactions included in an effective onboarding program will surface a "bad fit" much sooner. Without a formal onboarding process, a poor fit can go unnoticed for many months, costing the organization, department, hiring manager, and new hire precious productivity, reputation, time, and dollars. The wrong person in the job can also disrupt a team, its productivity, and may cause the loss of other valuable employees if left unaddressed.

From the Hiring Manager

This list of Perfect Phrases will signal that the hiring manager thinks the new hire may be a poor fit:

→ The jury is still out.

→ I thought her experience with (company) would be a real benefit, but now I'm not sure.

→ It is taking him longer than expected to get up to speed.

→ We have walked through our business model three times, and it doesn't seem to be sinking in.

→ It took us four months to fill this position—it needs to work out!

→ Our customers expect a (position title) who understands their business, and I'm not sure that (new hire) gets it.

→ I'm not sure what he's missing.

→ How do you think we can get him up to speed sooner rather than later?

→ I am hearing that he makes more statements than he asks questions—that's a problem.

→ We don't have the luxury of just onboarding for even 30 days.

→ Maybe we should have chosen an internal candidate.

→ (New hire) keeps talking about his previous company.

→ I am concerned.

→ I expected (new hire) to be ready.

→ Even after I have given (new hire) feedback about how we run our meetings, she still insists on doing it her way.

→ In our last onboarding meeting, it was clear that she still does not have a clear picture of her role here.

→ The feedback from his peers tells me that he is having a difficult time getting comfortable with our culture.

→ It's important to be prepared for our meetings, and she always seems a bit lost.

→ I need to talk to HR about (new hire).

→ Maybe we should have waited to fill the job.

→ (New hire) wants me to believe that he is building the right relationships, but that is not what I am hearing.

→ Our culture expects new hires to listen and learn; (new hire) has difficulty doing both.

→ It has been 60 days, and (new hire) still hasn't really connected with her coworkers.

From the HR Partner

These Perfect Phrases from the HR partner indicate that the new employee may be the wrong fit:

→ I have noticed (new employee) has not participated in any of our company events.

→ (New employee) seemed to be disengaged during our 60-day onboarding discussion.

→ Several of (new employee)'s onboarding objectives are more than 30 days overdue.

→ (New employee) was angry about the feedback from her peers that I shared with her. She listed all the reasons why the feedback was inaccurate.

→ (New employee)'s hiring manager has come to talk with me three times in the last 45 days to ask for help in onboarding her. He's definitely frustrated.

→ (New employee) told me that she has transitioned into new roles several times before and she does not need an onboarding plan.

→ I have reviewed (new employee)'s feedback report, and his peers seem to be frustrated with him.

→ (New employee)'s family is struggling to get integrated into the community.

→ I have noticed that (new employee) has not personalized her work space, and she's been here almost two months now.

→ (New employee) sent me an e-mail asking about the relocation policy and asked how long you need to stay with the organization to avoid having to repay the moving expenses.

→ (New employee) has cancelled the last two onboarding meetings that we have scheduled.

→ (New employee) told me that our culture is a lot different than she expected and she is having difficulty adjusting.

→ Our recruitment team did a great job persuading (new employee) to join us, but I am not sure that we have delivered on all of our promises.

→ (New employee)'s hiring manager has asked me about the "number two" candidate whom we identified during the search.

→ (New employee) met with me today and is frustrated with the lack of opportunity to demonstrate his abilities. Things are going too slow for him.

From the New Employee

These Perfect Phrases from the new associate indicate that she might not be a good fit for the role or the organization:

→ This is a lot different than I thought it would be.

→ I am still not clear what my job is after two months.

➜ My manager expects me to deliver already, and I haven't even been here a month yet.

➜ My onboarding plan includes several objectives to learn about the company, and I don't understand how they apply to my job.

➜ I have a lot of information technology (or insert other functional area) experience that I am not able to use here and I thought I would.

➜ My family doesn't seem to like this community compared to our old one.

➜ My manager gave me some feedback today about what I can do to fit in better, but I am not sure what to change.

➜ This is such a strong (strange) culture; it seems a bit over-the-top and not what I am used to.

➜ Things move much slower (faster) than in my previous company; I didn't expect that.

➜ During the selection process, I was told that I would get an office, and I have a cubicle instead.

➜ I thought that I could work a flextime schedule, and my manager said that she would think about it.

➜ Everyone keeps talking about the culture. I'm having a tough time figuring out what it is.

➜ I am feeling lonely here. Everyone in my department has strong relationships, and I can't see where I fit in.

➜ The recruiter who placed me in this job called me today; I think it's important to keep in touch with her.

→ My manager has been traveling 80% of the time since I started here, and we haven't had a chance to start to build any kind of relationship.

→ My manager left for another company during my second week. Now what?

During months 2 and 3, new employees are getting better integrated into the culture and have a clearer understanding of their roles. This is also the time period when certain behaviors start to surface that may signal a poor fit for some new hires either in a particular role or with the organization itself. Addressing these behaviors in this early stage will prevent long-term performance issues. Even if separation or termination is the final solution, this is a better outcome for both the new employee and the organization rather than delay the inevitable and create more disruption to the team or department.

CHAPTER

Perfect Phrases for Understanding the Culture

During the first months, the new employee starts to get glimpses (and sometimes fuller views) of what it is like to work inside the culture of the organization. The manager and the HR partner can help fill in the cultural information for the new employee to avoid confusion and conflict. These conversations should pick up right where they left off in the selection process. A key is to make sure that the employee talks about what is different about the culture from what she expected and what is consistent to what she expected based on her initial impressions.

The Culture Road Map

We have worked with clients to put together a culture road map. This resource gives new hires, hiring managers, and HR partners a coaching tool to use when talking about the organization's culture. This road map should reflect how the organization really works, makes decisions, deals with conflict, and so on. It is not the vision, mission, value statement, or what it hopes to be—i.e., the culture to which the company aspires. If the information is not real and doesn't reflect how people really work and behave, the new employee will make mistakes and may become frustrated and disillusioned.

Perfect Phrases for Creating a Culture Road Map

The answers to the following questions and phrases surface the organization's actual culture and provide the information that will make up the content of the culture road map.

→ Describe the "personality" of the organization.

→ List the five words that best describe the organization.

→ How are decisions made?

→ Tell me about a crisis that the company had to manage. What was the outcome?

→ What parts of the organization are core and have the most power?

→ List the most important processes in the company.

→ Outline the steps an employee should take for suggesting a new idea.

→ What are the unwritten rules for success?

→ A new hire should always _____.

→ A new hire should never _____.

→ The "sacred cows" in our organization are _____
   _____.

→ Tell me about the company's key customers.

→ What does it take to be successful in our organization?

→ The best advice for a new hire is _____
   _____.

→ Describe a situation when a new hire did a good job of navigating the culture.

→ Give an example of a situation when a new hire did not navigate the culture successfully.

These phrases are examples of what type of information is included in a culture road map that is a key resource document for your onboarding program.

Perfect Phrases for Success in the Company Culture

The following phrases are examples of typical behaviors that a new hire would try to use to successfully navigate the company culture.

→ At our company, we
   → Deliver
   → Are flexible
   → Are constructive ("I can")
   → Look for opportunities to innovate
   → Are honest (but not brutal)
   → Are accountable for mistakes
   → Do something (make a decision)
   → Keep the right people informed and involved (keep audience in mind)
   → Think of things from the customer's point of view
   → Communicate—there's a business reason

→ Focus on customer service

→ Stay on top of things

→ Assume that resources are scarce—don't assume that you can give work to a staff of people

→ Are flexible with roles and responsibilities

→ Have a sense of humor

Perfect Phrases for Things to Avoid in the Company Culture

The following phrases are examples of typical behaviors that new hires should be aware of and avoid in a new culture:

→ At our company, we don't

   → Say "I can't."

   → Say "This is the way we've always done it."

   → Try to cover up mistakes

   → Create negative surprises—never surprise leadership, coworkers, or customers

   → Wait for perfection

   → Take a media call directly

   → Disclose financial information externally

   → Tarnish the company by sacrificing customer service

   → Ignore requests (especially from customers)

   → Assume our roles will stay the same

   → Accept or decline a job because of who our manager would be

- → Say "That's not my job!"
- → Take all the credit
- → Pull rank—we are all accountable to each other

Remember, it is critical to make these phrases "your own" so that they truly represent the actual, true culture of your organization!

Perfect Phrases to Understand the Culture

Many times new employees, and especially new leaders, are expected to "meet and greet" a great many people during their first weeks on the job. These Perfect Phrases give the new employee key questions to use in conversations and meetings with a wide variety of key stakeholders, both inside and outside the organization. Examples include the new hire's manager, peers, direct reports, internal clients, external clients, and suppliers, as appropriate.

- → How would you describe our organization?
- → When you talk about where you work to those outside of the organization, what do you say?
- → Tell me about your role here.
- → What do you like about the company and its culture?
- → Tell me about some of the barriers you have at our company.
- → What motivates you about working here?

→ I am interested in knowing how our functions (departments) are working together.

→ It seems important for our teams to work together. How could our functions (departments) do a better job of coordinating work?

→ What are your objectives for the next (quarter, season, year)?

→ How can my function (department) support yours?

→ What advice do you have for me?

→ How are decisions made in this organization?

→ Which parts of the organization have the most clout?

→ What happens when there is conflict?

→ How is most communication done here?

→ What type of communication do you prefer?

→ How long is a person considered "new" in this company?

→ What are the "sacred cows" here?

→ What are the unwritten rules for being successful in this organization?

→ What do we always do? Never do?

→ What does the company value?

→ How do you know what is important here?

→ Is it more important to deliver results or put in "face time" at the office? Or both?

→ Generally, how much time do people put in here?

→ Is it acceptable to work flexible hours?

→ Is working from home OK?

→ Please share some examples of how we are recognized and rewarded.

→ What is important here, and how do you know it's important?

→ Describe the process for effectively "selling" an idea here.

→ Do people go out to eat for lunch?

→ Is it OK to eat at your desk (work space)?

→ Can we use the (mailroom, copier, fax) for personal items?

→ How can I get (temporary help, training, travel approval) when I need it?

→ What are some of the things you wish you had known when you were new?

Perfect Phrases from the Hiring Manager to Encourage Success in the Culture

The hiring manager and/or HR partner play a key role in helping the new employee understand and adapt to the culture of the organization. These "getting the culture" phrases hold true for most organizations, but it is important to change them to reflect the actual culture of a particular organization as these coaching opportunities present themselves.

Input from a hiring manager should be focused on the department and the role as well as the broader organization. The hiring manager has the unique perspective of a line manager responsible for leading her team and delivering results. She is also the individual who will be evaluating the onboarding success and longer-term performance of the new hire.

→ Observe everything and try not to judge whether it is the "right" or "wrong" way to do it.

→ Assume nothing, ask.

→ Watch and listen.

→ Remember there is usually more than one "right answer."

→ If you make a mistake, find out why and how to improve.

→ Speak up (or listen carefully) at the meetings you attend.

→ Make sure that you are clear about your role and performance expectations for your first 30, 60, and 90 days.

→ We are pretty formal (informal) here, so your communication needs to look like_____.

→ The way we use e-mail is _____.

→ Deliver on your commitments.

→ Expect surprises about your role, your partners, and the organization.

→ If you have a new idea, the best way to "sell it" is to _____
_____.

→ Make sure that you understand the history and ownership of anything that you want to change.

→ Early on, avoid high-risk initiatives; find "early wins" or "quick hits" to establish credibility.

→ It's OK (not OK) to be late for meetings.

Perfect Phrases from the HR Partner to Encourage Success in the Culture

The HR partner responsible for supporting a new hire through the onboarding process has a broad view of the organization's culture. An HR partner can also serve as a safe person to ask questions that a new hire may not be comfortable asking others. In addition, the HR partner is also a great resource for the new hire to use to better understand her hiring manager.

→ Get to know the administrative assistants—they know a lot!

→ Take advantage of being "new."

→ The most important thing you need to know about our culture is _____.

→ Look for ways to get to know people away from work.

→ Participate in all the company events that you can.

→ Some key people who can help you with our culture are

_____.

→ Identify the people, both in and out of the organization, with whom you need to build relationships. I have made a draft list to get you started.

→ Look up, down, and sideways for the people you need to get to know.

→ Some of the most important people in your network might be in other departments or functions in the organization.

→ Manage the expectations of your manager, your team, and your customers.

→ The way we use social media (Facebook, LinkedIn, Twitter) here is _____.

→ Use your onboarding process and resources to manage the surprises.

→ Ask lots of questions and actively listen as you learn.

→ We encourage you to be curious about everything you do, especially as you are getting to know people and learning about our business.

→ Pay attention to how people respond to both the positive and the negative.

→ Learn the quirks of our culture, because what works in one place can look and feel different in another.

→ Ask other people to share one piece of advice, words of wisdom, or lessons learned with you in the spirit of helping you onboard as efficiently as you can.

→ Give priority to your manager's priorities.

→ Respect the culture and learn all you can before suggesting or making changes.

→ Understand the organization's politics and work with it.

→ Decision making here is pretty _____ (consensus based, relationship based, data driven, financially driven, autocratic, etc.), so the best way to navigate this process is _____ _____.

→ Respond appropriately to the unexpected, to conflict, and to disagreement.

Remember what is said, "Culture eats strategy for breakfast." Generally, it is not the work that will trip up a new employee, but the culture. It is common especially for employees who have been successful to continue to behave in ways that made them successful in their former cultures. They do not or will not make the necessary adjustments to the new culture, and then they have problems. So early feedback is critical. (See Chapter 10 for more on how to give feedback about integrating into the culture.) If you take the time to create and integrate a culture road map into your onboarding program, it will provide a coaching tool for your hiring managers, HR partners, and all your new employees and help them be successful.

CHAPTER 8

Month 4: Perfect Phrases for Typical Onboarding Challenges

No one's onboarding experience is perfect. There are always bumps in the road and challenges to work through. This is true for a seasoned executive, a newly promoted manager, and a new college grad, and it is important for all to have someone in the organization with whom they can talk openly and honestly to manage the rough spots. Common onboarding challenges include generally being overwhelmed, lack of role clarity, culture issues, being a part of a geographically dispersed team, or having a disengaged manager, just to name a few. With the help of a trusted adviser who can be the manager, a peer, or an HR partner, the new employee can get the guidance and the reality check that she may need. All new employees experience some type of a "the honeymoon is over" phenomenon or culture shock when they enter an organization. Everyone needs feedback and coaching during the onboarding experience, especially when there are roadblocks and challenges. The best course to take is to address the challenges as they occur with open acknowledgment and a true interest in helping the new employee get resolution before it's too late.

Perfect Phrases to Coach a New Employee Through Onboarding Challenges

Usually reality hits at about the 30- or 40-day mark. The new hire now understands more about the role she accepted. Although her intellectual knowledge about the job, the organization, and her relationships is increasing each day, her emotions are on a roller coaster and fluctuate depending on the day, week, or month. These Perfect Phrases may be used by the HR partner or manager as she is coaching the new employee through typical onboarding challenges and general onboarding ups and downs.

→ Research shows that as your knowledge about your job and organization continues to grow, your emotions will be up and down depending on what is happening during that time period.

→ Manage the highs and lows of being new by recognizing that you can't and won't know everything in two or three months.

→ It probably takes between 12 and 18 months for a new employee to be fully integrated into a new role and a new culture.

→ Ask for help when you need it. Don't wait until things are really bad or until you are so frustrated that it will take more effort to correct the situation than it needed to.

→ Most everyone "hits a wall" at about month 3 or 4. How are you feeling about your decision to take this role?

→ I get the sense that you are hitting some barriers. Let's talk about it.

→ It can take anywhere from 12 to 18 months to be fully onboarded, so be patient.

→ Ups and downs are completely normal during onboarding.

→ I have heard that you are frustrated with _____. What's going on?

→ You seem a little "off." Do you want to talk about it?

Perfect Phrases for Issues of Role Clarity

Studies continue to validate that a lack of role clarity is one of the leading reasons that leads to derailment for a new employee. Too often hiring managers assume that their new employees are in alignment with them and don't take the time to talk about this enough as roles evolve.

→ Your role might be different than you expected it to be, so identify the differences and talk with your manager about those gaps.

→ I understand that you feel like this is not what you "signed up for." Let's talk about what's different.

→ Almost everyone feels like the job he or she accepted is different from the one that he or she is doing. What does your manager say?

→ I know that your manager said _____ in your selection process, but things have changed. Let's talk about it.

Perfect Phrases for Issues with Expectations and Results

Assumptions from conversations in the selection process are often the culprit to onboarding challenges here. Having a clear onboarding plan with time-based objectives will also take the guesswork out and address the gaps.

→ Trying to do too much too soon can be too much too soon. Trying to make a good impression and being too "heroic" in expectations can be stressful and can actually lead to alienating others instead of building relationships.

→ Take on reasonable expectations.

→ We are a lean organization, and we do expect you to deliver results at the same time that you are learning our organization.

→ Acting like you have all the "right answers" can make you seem arrogant, and you will have a difficult time building relationships and gaining support for your initiatives.

Perfect Phrases for Issues of Change

Being hired as a change agent is a tough assignment. Many organizations expect some of their new employees, particularly at the leadership level, to fulfill this role. It can be done, but again, within the context of the culture and what the organization will support.

➜ Changes are easier to make when you have built strong relationships. Let's talk about who you need to get to know better.

➜ I understand that "change" was a big theme during your selection process and that you are ready to implement some new things; however, it is important to know the best way to initiate change in our organization.

➜ Your team has been through a great deal of transition lately; let's talk about doing a working session to surface some of their concerns.

Perfect Phrases for Issues of Time Management

Perceptions of how a new employee is spending his time will affect how he is accepted in the culture. It is important to coach him appropriately as soon as problematic behaviors are noticed.

→ Prioritize and be structured, but stay flexible for unexpected demands. Don't schedule more than about 60% of your day so that you can respond to other things. This will also reduce stress and make you more accessible.

→ Manage your time wisely, and observe how others who do this well manage their time.

→ I am concerned that you have cancelled our last few onboarding meetings. Let's talk about how we can stay in touch.

Perfect Phrases for Issues with the Manager

The most important first relationship is that with the hiring manager. This relationship will set the tone and future success or failure of the new employee, so it's critical to talk about issues as they arise.

→ Your manager does travel a lot; maybe you can set up regular conference calls to stay in touch.

→ Your manager's style is different from your style. What do you know about her that will help you communicate successfully?

→ Here are some things I know about your manager that might help you as you get to know each other.

→ I know that your manager said _____ in your selection process, but things have changed. Let's talk about it.

Perfect Phrases for Issues with the Culture

Culture continues to be one of the most significant transition issues for all new employees. Refer to Chapter 7 for a more in-depth discussion on how culture affects onboarding.

→ It can take new employees up to a full year to really "get" the culture in our organization. What are some examples of the issues that have come up for you?

→ This culture can be tough. Here's what worked for me:
_____.

→ Our culture can sometimes be tricky for new hires. What feedback have you gotten?

→ Let's talk about how you can act on the feedback you've received so far.

→ Here's what I know about the culture you came from at _____, and here is how I see it as different from the culture here. What do you think?

→ Let's talk about the best ways to navigate now that we know what the concerns are.

Perfect Phrases for Issues with Personal Transition and Relocation

In a study we conducted, we found that approximately 65 percent of the issues in retention of new employees were related to personal transition. The types of issues that they included were spouses who were unable to find employment or were unhappy with the new community, or children not adjusting to the new schools or community. Although most organizations are not comfortable talking about this topic and "mixing" personal with professional lives, it does affect their ability to recruit and retain top talent.

→ If your family (significant other) is not happy with your transition, we can brainstorm some solutions, and then let me help you put a plan together.

→ _____ in the department (organization) had some experiences similar to this when he moved and started his job here. I can ask him if he would be willing to share some of his advice and experiences with you.

→ This community is different from the one you came from, and I can understand how you and your family are feeling. What are you missing the most? What are some things that you enjoy that we can help get you connected to here?

→ What else can I do to support you and your family?

→ Who else can you talk with about this?

→ Have you talked to your manager (HR partner)?

Coaching new employees as soon as the onboarding challenges surface is the best way to prevent derailment and potential long-term performance and behavior issues that can lead to derailment. This feedback and guidance is also critical for keeping new hires highly engaged. It is common for new employees to disengage once they face some of these typical challenges and if their managers or HR partners are not proactive and have the appropriate conversations with them to work through these trouble spots. These new employees risk failure. Regardless of level or position, years of experience, or knowledge of the role, all new employees experience some type of barrier, setback, or cultural clash in their first months on the job. Anticipate these challenges, and use the Perfect Phrase to work to get them back on track.

CHAPTER 9

Perfect Phrases for Collecting Onboarding Feedback

Onboarding feedback as part of a structured onboarding process is different from performance feedback. It allows the new employee to see specifically how he is or isn't integrating into the culture of the organization. Onboarding feedback is not only about the deliverables of the job and the metrics that are typically used in performance management. This doesn't mean, however, that the feedback is not data oriented. Surveys and conversations that occur between days 45 and 60 can collect hard evidence of how a new employee is transitioning and integrating into the job.

Sometimes we get push-back from organizations that say 45 to 60 days is too soon to collect onboarding feedback. Our response is that perceptions and impressions of the new employee have already been made during the selection process and the first days on the job. These impressions and perceptions are what make up this early feedback, and it is in the best interest of the new employee to get that information as soon as possible. Only then will she be able to make corrections that allow her to be more successful and not continue to make mistakes that could be harder to correct down the road.

Perfect Phrases for Building Feedback into the Onboarding Program

→ Research shows that onboarding programs that include feedback produce employees who are more engaged.

→ By matching your metrics and measurements to the objectives of your onboarding process, you are more likely to achieve them.

→ Build the collection of data into onboarding actions like structured conversations and time-based surveys.

→ Ask questions that collect data about the progress of the individual as well as the success (or failure) of the onboarding process. For example, ask the employee if he or she would agree or disagree with the following statements: "1. My manager met with me the first week to explain my onboarding plan. 2. My office was set up and my computer and phone were working."

→ Collect quantitative and qualitative feedback data (for example, use a numeric scale as well as a comments section on a survey).

→ Key milestones to target for collecting new employee feedback are at the end of week 1, at the end of month 1, at the midpoint of your formal onboarding program, and at the completion of your onboarding program.

→ Include all the participants in the onboarding experience: the manager, peers, direct reports, HR partner, customers, and the new employee for a self-assessment.

→ Build in some of the same questions into conversations and surveys that are used by the manager and the HR partner with the new employee. Collecting the same data from different participants yields rich results.

→ Report results by individual, by hiring manager, by department, by function, by business unit, and by organization to track trends.

→ Use the feedback data to make adjustments to your overall onboarding program.

→ The feedback data can also be used to measure ROI for your onboarding process investment.

Perfect Phrases for Collecting Onboarding Feedback

These phrases are effective on a written survey or in a feedback conversation with key stakeholders. Use a multi-rater format that includes the manager, peers, direct reports, customers, and others who interact with the new employee. These are particularly effective feedback questions for new leaders and managers, but they can be used and adapted to fit employees at any level in the organization.

→ Does/is the new employee
  → Actively listen?
  → Assess each situation on its own and usually not have preconceived ideas?

- → Build relationships to overcome resistance and achieve results?
- → Build the foundation for change before taking action?
- → Deal with small problems as effectively as big problems?
- → Deliver on commitments?
- → Demonstrate an appropriate level of humility?
- → Fit into the team?
- → Execute well on task and initiatives—deliver results?
- → Identify and continuously build the right relationships?
- → Aware of personal blind spots?
- → More interested in learning about the company and his or her role than focusing on impressing others?
- → Manage time effectively?
- → Rely on a variety of skills, and not overuse strengths?
- → Seek input?
- → Understand organizational politics?
- → Understand and fulfill the expectations of his or her role?
- → Understand and respect company culture?
- → Use technical skills in a way that is appropriate for the job?
- → What two or three things does this person do that makes him or her most effective?

➜ What should this person change, do differently, or do less of to make him or her more effective?

➜ What recommendations do you have for further supporting this person's onboarding?

It may be helpful to include a numeric rating scale for each of these areas so that the rater and the new employee have a quantitative and qualitative rating for each behavior. The last three questions are designed to be open-ended to generate specific suggestions and actions for the new employee as he or she makes adjustments in his or her onboarding plan.

CHAPTER 10

Perfect Phrases for Giving Onboarding Feedback

I t is critical to collect feedback about the behaviors and perceptions of a new employee, and it is equally important to deliver that feedback so that the new employee can first understand it and then be able to act on. Managers tend to shy away from giving feedback because they fear or dislike conflict or the perceived negative feelings that feedback can produce for the receiver. Our view is that feedback is really a gift. People are thinking and feeling this way, so give the new employee a chance to hear it and then make changes. These changes could in fact be the ones that "save" the employee in his or her new role.

Perfect Phrases to Coach a New Employee on Constructive or Negative Feedback

Use these Perfect Phrases to coach a new employee when he or she gets constructive or negative feedback in one or more of the following areas.

When the Employee Is Not Actively Listening

→ Are you asking enough questions about the organization, your colleagues, their work, and how your team is serving them?

→ Has listening more or less always been a challenge? Now more than ever, active listening is an important skill to demonstrate. Taking notes can help.

→ Let people know you're hearing them. Some ways to do this include summarizing back what you've just heard, paraphrasing, and mirroring concerns or key points.

→ Are you in a hurry to prove yourself? Remember that this can be a key derailer or disconnect. Slow down and learn.

When the Employee Does Not Size Up a Situation or Has Preconceived Ideas

→ It is very tempting in today's fast-paced business environment to want to size things up quickly and respond decisively. Remember that you are operating in a new business context, and even if you've experienced a similar situation in the past, it doesn't mean the solution that worked before will work again.

→ Take the time to do a thorough search for information, including asking people what they think the solution should be and about solutions that have failed in the past.

When the Employee Is Not Building Relationships (to Overcome Resistance)

→ Have you identified all of your key stakeholders?

→ It is crucial to understand what's important to each of your stakeholders.

→ Identify what your common goals are with each individual stakeholder.

→ Do you know how you, together, support organizational success? This common ground can become the basis for engaging their support.

→ What can you do to help them be successful?

→ Are you behaving in a way that might undermine relationship building?

When the Employee Fails to Build a Foundation for Change Before Taking Action

→ Were you put in your role specifically to enact change? If so, you still need to "earn the right" to bring about those changes through developing the support of others.

→ Have you done a thorough search for information before trying to make these changes?

→ How well do you understand, and demonstrate respect for, the organization as it was before you got here?

→ Based on what you have learned, have you been able to develop credibility by showing that it is relevant in our organization?

→ Make sure that your ideas make sense in the current business context.

→ How do the people who are most affected by the change feel about the changes you want to make?

→ What will it take to move them from opposing your ideas to supporting them?

When the Employee Is Not Handling Small Problems as Effectively as Big Ones

→ What are you learning from the problems you're encountering in your new role?

→ What do these problems tell you about your team and the organization?

→ Are you asking how the organization has handled similar problems in the past and how they turned out?

For New Leaders

→ Are you taking the time to accurately size up the problems you face, and are you delegating them in a way that maps them onto the skills of your team and/or their development needs?

→ Do you think certain problems are "beneath you"? As a new manager, you might be missing key opportunities to learn the work and develop or strengthen relationships.

When the Employee Is Not Delivering on Commitments

→ What commitments have you "inherited" in your new role?

→ Are they realistic?

→ If not, what can you do to realign expectations?

→ Are you missing resources to help you? What are they?

→ Have you made realistic commitments to others since joining your role?

→ Is your team equipped to deliver on them? If not, what actions must be taken to make it happen?

When the Employee Does Not Show Appropriate Humility

→ Are you really good at what you do? Do other people know that you think so? That could be a problem if you are being perceived as overly confident before you have formed relationships here.

→ Have you come into your job with all the right "answers"? Or have you been smart enough to come in with all the right questions?

→ It may feel risky not to know everything when you are new, but research shows that people who adopt this approach are more likely to be successful long-term. This is a great opportunity to build relationships and gain support.

When the Employee Is Not Fitting into the Team

➜ What is different about how you are behaving compared to the other team members?

➜ What have you noticed as successful ways to interact with the team?

➜ What have been some not so successful ways?

➜ What is the impact?

➜ Let's talk about some strategies to get back on track.

When the Employee Is Not Delivering Results

➜ What results are you expected to deliver?

➜ What is the timeline/deadline for these?

➜ Are you and your manager aligned with what your deliverables are? When was the last time you checked?

For Leaders

➜ At your level, most results are delivered through your team. How well do you understand their work and how it fits with your key deliverables?

➜ What gaps exist?

➜ Have you sized up your team to understand their strengths and weaknesses?

➜ What have you done to validate this information and understanding?

➜ What do you need to do to close the gaps?

➜ How long do you have?

When the Employee Is Having Difficulty Identifying and Building Relationships

→ Have you done a thorough stakeholder analysis?

→ Have you had a chance to meet with your key stakeholders to discuss topics that are important to both of you?

→ After your initial conversations, what have you done to create or continue momentum in the relationship?

→ Are you following up in your communication?

→ Are you making a point to deliver on your commitments?

→ What have you done to identify and build upon or support your key stakeholders' priorities? (It's a good idea to offer help before being asked.)

When the Employee Is Not Aware of His or Her Blind Spots

→ The recruitment process often centers on candidate strengths and fails to address areas of potential concern or development needs. Do you know what yours are?

→ How do they fit with what's needed in the organization?

→ Have they been validated by your new manager?

→ What's your plan to use your strengths and work on your development needs?

→ What does the organization expect you to do?

→ What organizational resources could you use for gaining additional feedback and developmental support?

When the Employee Is Less Interested in Learning Than in Impressing Others

→ It is important that others get to know you and your skills. What matters most to them, however, is that you understand the organization and the job (especially before trying to bring about changes).

→ Sure, they hired you because you're good. And they'll see that, if you give them enough time.

→ Nothing personal, but people are not usually interested in hearing how you handled a similar situation in your old organization—at least not until they think you've done your due diligence in your new one.

→ Once you understand your new environment, it will be much easier to create a positive impression of your contributions.

When the Employee Is Not Managing Time Effectively

→ What are the expected working hours?

→ How do your hours compare to those of others?

→ On what are you spending your time?

→ How does this align with the priorities that your manager outlined for you?

→ What is getting in the way for you to be more effective at this?

→ Do meetings start and end on time? What's the cadence of a typical meeting?

→ Is it OK to be late? How late? Whose meetings?

→ Self-manage, and be very respectful of the time of others. It may take a few weeks, but you'll get into the rhythm.

When the Employee Does Not Rely on a Variety of Skills

→ It's important to recognize which specific skills are needed for a particular situation.

→ How do you make these decisions?

→ What other strengths can you draw on to get a solution?

→ Have you identified what skills and strengths the others on the team can bring to the table?

→ Who else on your team can work with you?

→ Are there additional resources that would help you complement what you currently have?

When the Employee Is Not Seeking Input

→ How do your key work deliverables support the overall department and organization?

→ What impact do they have on the work of others?

→ How can you learn more about this?

→ What are your deliverables that require the input of others?

→ How have you been approaching seeking input?

→ How have you incorporated their suggestions and addressed their concerns?

➔ How have you communicated when you found you could not incorporate their ideas or address their concerns?

➔ What else may not require the input of others but could be implemented more quickly or effectively with their buy-in?

➔ Are you seeking input in those situations?

When the Employee Is Having Difficulty with Organizational Politics

➔ People, especially new leaders, often dislike organizational politics, but they are a fact of life and represent the unique needs of all your work relationships.

➔ Do you understand your key stakeholders' "hot buttons," and are you willing and able to navigate in a way that takes their perspectives into account?

➔ Are you able to step back from situations and see them rationally, even if your colleague(s) may make it challenging?

➔ Do you respond rather than react, addressing both businesses' needs while at the same time addressing their concerns?

➔ Do you communicate if you are unable to address their concerns while serving business needs?

When the Employee Doesn't Understand the Expectations of the Role

→ Do you know what is expected of you in terms of short- and long-term performance goals?

→ Do you know the purpose of your role?

→ When's the last time you confirmed/adjusted your role with your manager?

→ What's happening in the organization (or could happen) that might affect your direction?

→ How have you communicated any changes in direction/ expectation with your key relationships and teams? If you do not do so, they will hold you to their old expectations (and can reduce your effectiveness).

→ How do you keep others informed about the status of your deliverables?

When the Employee Doesn't Understand or Respect Company Culture

→ Have you taken the time to get to know your new organization?

→ What "makes it tick"?

→ How do people get the work done?

→ What are the stories about why things are done the way they are?

➔ What do successful people always do?

➔ What do they never do?

➔ Have you learned these "rules of the road" quickly and thoroughly?

➔ What other information do you need that will help you learn?

➔ It is also really important to get feedback on how you are doing.

When the Employee Is Not Using Technical Skills in a Way That Is Appropriate for the Job

➔ Are you an expert in your area? Do you have deep technical skills? Some new hires, particularly new leaders, like to learn their roles by diving deep into the technical aspects of the work. This is not a bad thing, but it definitely should be just a phase of the transition.

➔ Or, are you new to your area or without deep skills in that area? Concentrating on learning the technical side of the work may be a good investment of time for you.

➔ Identify a couple of subject matter experts and spend time with them to learn the ins and outs of the work your team does.

Perfect Phrases to Deliver Onboarding Feedback to the New Employee

Remember that how you have the feedback conversation with the new employee is just as important as what you say during that meeting. These Perfect Phrases can help prepare the HR partner who is an experienced feedback coach to deliver the onboarding feedback data to the new employee:

Prior to the Feedback Meeting

→ Make sure you are fully briefed about all the details of the particular feedback process.

→ Review the feedback report, looking for major patterns and themes. Spend no more than 20 minutes reviewing the report, otherwise you risk overinterpretation. Your role is to facilitate, not to diagnose. You cannot interpret a feedback report without the participant.

→ Schedule enough time for the meeting depending on the amount of feedback and circumstances.

→ Find a quiet, private place like a conference room, not an office where there are distractions of phones, computers, e-mails, and coworkers, and plan for a one- to two-hour meeting.

→ Communicate the purpose of the meeting to the employee who is receiving the feedback.

At the Beginning of the Meeting

→ Confirm the purpose of the feedback component of the onboarding program, explain how the feedback report will be used and that it is confidential. Outline the role of the facilitator and explain the session process. Be assertive, specific, and supportive at all times.

→ Reinforce that feedback is simply a collection of perceptions. Assess the levels of defensiveness in the participant's body language and verbal responses. Concentrate on establishing rapport if there is evidence of resistance to feedback.

→ Ask the participant who was in the rating team. Explain that the participant is likely to find the feedback useful and interesting. It is your role to ensure that the session is constructive.

→ Ask the participant to list three of his or her strengths and three challenges he or she faces in the current role.

→ Ask the participant to describe his or her relationship with the manager and team.

→ Spend no more than 5 to 10 minutes on this introductory activity, as participants will be anxious to explore the report.

During the Meeting

→ Ask clarifying questions to stimulate insights.

→ Use tentative/hypothetical language when building a picture with the participant.

→ Observe and provide feedback about visible behaviors linked to the report.

→ Provide support and encouragement—lead with the positives.

→ Help the participant to identify key themes within the report. What are some of the overall messages?

→ Identify major gaps and similarities between the self-ratings and the perceptions of others.

→ Focus only on behaviors, not on personality.

→ Try to make sure that the participant is providing most of the comments.

At the End of the Meeting

→ Brainstorm options for improvement and development.

→ Develop a few specific actions that can be the basis of an action/development plan.

→ Ask the participant for feedback about the process.

→ Thank the participant.

Follow-Up

→ Encourage the participant to have a follow-up meeting with his or her manager. Participants usually have questions about the ratings given to them by their managers. It is also important for the managers to be involved in the ongoing development plans.

→ Encourage the participant to give his or her rating team some feedback about what he or she learned in the feedback process.

Perfect Phrases to Prepare the New Employee to Receive Onboarding Feedback

These phrases may be used in an e-mail or a conversation with the new employee to prepare her for the feedback conversation. It allows the new hire to anticipate constructive feedback and be able to receive it so that she is open to it and understands the messages. This preparation will minimize the tendency to be defensive and encourages the new employee to be an active participant in the discussion.

Prior to the Feedback Meeting

→ Write down your personal idea of success in the workplace.

→ Reflect on how you could be more effective.

→ Consider your current level of job satisfaction. What things are negatively impacting your commitment?

→ Consider how open you are to knowing how your actions might affect others.

→ Ask yourself how willing you are to accept the perceptions of others, even if you do not agree with them.

At the Beginning of the Meeting

→ Make sure you have a nondefensive and open attitude. It sounds easy, but it can be hard to maintain under stress.

→ Relax and treat the session as an interesting exploration. The potential for learning is high.

→ Make sure all distractions have been removed and that you are able to focus on the process.

During the Meeting

→ Develop an overview of the report. Try to identify key themes and patterns.

→ When a particular rating puzzles you, try to think about how that perception may have been formed.

→ Look for differences in ratings from different groups. When gaps are evident, ask yourself if you behave differently with different groups.

→ How do you tend to rate yourself? Are you overly harsh or generous?

At the End of the Meeting

→ Identify a few key points and related actions.

→ Brainstorm appropriate development opportunities or commit to researching them.

→ Consider if you have had similar feedback before in your career.

Follow-Up

→ There are likely to be unanswered questions, and the reflection process will continue over the next week. Make sure that you set aside some time for reflection and discussions with key individuals to help the clarification process.

→ Thank your rating team and give them some feedback.

→ Involve your manager in your development plan.

→ Revisit your feedback report and action/development
   plan at regular intervals during the year.

The power of feedback cannot be underestimated. In most
cases, new employees are concerned about proving themselves
and doing well, so they very often are not aware if they are exhib-
iting behaviors that aren't fitting into the culture unless someone tells them. Too often, people do talk about these behaviors,
just not directly to the new employee!

CHAPTER 11

Perfect Phrases for Onboarding a Diverse Workforce

At this time, like no other, the workplace is a diverse mix of genders, socioeconomic backgrounds, races, religions, management styles, and age demographics. The news for organizations about five years ago was to get ready for the great exodus of the baby boomer generation from the workforce and the huge void it would create in the talent pool. However, the economy had its own ideas, and with the recession, kept many more boomers working than most had probably originally planned. This presents organizations with a "good news–bad news" situation. The good news is that much of their talent and knowledge did not retire and they now have the opportunity to transfer it to the next generation of workers. They also have the opportunity to hire older, more experienced workers who bring valuable resources and knowledge from previous employers. The "bad news" is that organizations need to flex their programs and experiences, like orientation and onboarding, to fit the needs of all of the generations now represented in most organizations.

Here is a quick review of the definitions that we will use for the common generational groupings:

Baby boomers: The generation born after World War II through 1960.

Generation X: The generation born from 1961 through 1981.

Generation Y (or Millennials): The generation born 1982 and after.

Perfect Phrases for Onboarding Baby Boomers

Boomers are the dominant generational group in the workforce, but not necessarily the dominant group that is onboarding. They are, however, the largest group in the workforce today. The boomers were expected to be leaving their jobs in droves by now and retiring, but the recent economic changes have kept them in place. They will find themselves in the minority, however, with Gen Xers and Gen Ys in orientation and onboarding, and will respond differently based on their backgrounds and experiences. Because baby boomers embrace the corporate structure, are comfortable with formality, want to be in charge, and love to win, they have very different needs as it relates to supporting their successful orientation and onboarding.

→ Welcome! We are lucky to have you with your knowledge and experience.

→ It's great to have someone on board who knows (understands) the industry.

→ The reason we hired you for this role is _____
_____.

→ Our organization is probably similar to what you know in these ways: _____.

→ Our organization is somewhat different from what you may be used to in these ways: _____.

→ You will participate in a half-day orientation program on your first day, then move into a formal onboarding period for 90 days.

→ Here is how you are doing compared to your onboarding plan: _____.

→ What I see you have delivered versus what I have expected from you in your first 90 days is _____.

→ Let's talk about your progress on your onboarding objectives.

→ Tell me about some of your "early wins" or "quick hits" that you have accomplished to establish some early credibility.

→ Now that you have been successful with _____ _____, let's add this next piece: _____.

→ Communication in our organization is mostly (face-to-face, e-mail, voice mail, whichever apply).

→ The ways in which you were successful in your previous role may not always happen for you here. Let's talk about the differences.

→ We have a collaborative culture, so it is important that you communicate with the team throughout the whole process. For example, meeting notes, pre-meeting conversations, and post-meeting debriefings are expected.

→ One thing to consider as you work on that project is to be inclusive and be clear about each person's role and responsibilities.

→ We have a very lean organization, and here is what that means for your role: _____.

Perfect Phrases for Onboarding Generation Xers

What we know about the Xers is that they feel rather "squeezed" between the baby boomers and the Gen Ys. There are fewer of them, by sheer numbers, than in either of the other two groups, so they are always in the minority. They also are now of the age when they are often responsible for younger children at home and may not be as mobile, and so may be less able to take promotions that require relocations, or less willing to work late hours or participate in social after-work activities. This can lead to some type of additional separation among the groups. Gen X also grew up in a world where downsizing and mismanagement were common, and so they don't often trust the "corporate-speak." Gen X highly values having options, and options often trump money or status. They tend to resent the boomers who see their way as the only way, and the fact that the boomers are hanging around in the workplace a lot longer than anyone thought they would, especially in leadership roles. However, Gen X brings strong relationships into the workplace and teaches others how to leverage them for powerful results. They also embrace technology as they have practically grown up with the personal computer and the cell phone. They are also not afraid of change as it relates to the work world, because it has done nothing but change since they entered it. They appreciate diversity and understand its value; they are instinctively collaborative, are usually quite flexible, and tend to ask questions instead of making statements as their boomer counterparts do.

→ Welcome! We are so glad to have you as part of our team!

→ The reason that we see you fitting in here so well is _____
_____.

→ Some of the strengths that you bring to our organization are _____.

→ A couple of the things that may be a challenge for you here are _____.

→ We have a plan to make your first months on the job successful, and you will drive it.

→ Our onboarding program will allow you to set objectives and learn the organization at the same time you build relationships along the way.

→ Your onboarding experience will allow for learning not only your particular role and function, but also our organization's culture, core processes, and customer experience.

→ Relationships are key here. Let's talk about the ones you have started already and how to grow them, and then build a plan for the ones that you will need to develop.

→ We strive for a structured, yet flexible onboarding experience tailored to meet you where you are, where you've been, and where you are going in the future.

→ We have the ability to work flexible hours in our organization. Here is where you can find some additional information about that: _____.

→ If you are interested in meeting with some of the other newer employees, here is how you can connect with them: _____.

→ We are committed to your career development, and your onboarding plan is the first piece. We will start with your onboarding plan and work with you to implement it.

→ What's your cell number? Here is mine _____ if you need anything.

→ Communication in our organization is mostly (face-to-face, e-mail, voice mail, whichever apply).

→ Feedback is an important part of our process too. Here's how you will get it: _____.

→ Your onboarding plan will serve as a springboard for your development plan, and this is how they will fit together:

_____.

→ As you start to meet people, here are some suggested topics to engage them:

   → How our teams work together
   → What the biggest opportunities are
   → What the barriers are

Perfect Phrases for Onboarding Generation Y, or the Millennials

Generation Y, or the Millennials, are technology kids and the ones who are the most comfortable with a global, multicultural world. They also have a reputation of being high maintenance, requiring instant gratification, and being skeptical. They have also, like their Gen X cousins, seen their parents and grandparents downsized and laid off, so their loyalties to corporate entities are few. On the other hand, they have high expectations of themselves for work output and usually put their families and personal lives over their work lives. They can be effective multitaskers and are extremely flexible. They do, however, demand flexibility from their employers because for them it is all about the work and not about how many hours it takes to get it done. Organizations can benefit from these hard workers but must manage them carefully and appropriately. Red flags for onboarding Generation Y include their "helicopter parents" inserting themselves into the process that may not be appropriate and entitlement signals that should be addressed immediately.

→ Welcome! So glad you are joining us!

→ It's great to have you as part of our team!

→ So glad you're here!

→ We really appreciate your energy and enthusiasm.

→ It can be a big transition from campus to the corporate world. There is a group that meets every week to talk through some common issues, and there are some additional resources available on our intranet.

→ We have clear policies about travel, expenses, temporary housing, compensation and benefits, attendance, etc. I can help direct you to the information. Do you have specific questions?

→ HR can give you some more information on how to interpret our dress code—sometimes it is tricky to understand what "business casual" actually means.

→ There is more info about our organization at www._____ _____ (or I will send you a link).

→ Our intranet, learning management system (LMS), or video library might be of interest to you. Here is a link to get you started: _____.

→ What's your cell number? Here is mine _____ if you need anything.

→ The best way to meet people in our organization is through _____.

→ Onboarding is an important part of your career development, and you will lead the way with our support.

→ Your manager will help you build a plan that will guide your first 90 days and outline your onboarding objectives.

→ We are committed to your career development and want you to drive the process. We have started your plan, but we expect you to drive it.

→ We want you to be able to learn and work at the same time.

→ Promotions will come as you develop and when they are appropriate. We can always have a conversation about what you want to accomplish next.

➜ Communication in our organization is mostly (face-to-face, e-mail, voice mail, whichever apply).

➜ The way we use social media in our organization is pretty formal, and it looks like _____.

➜ The way we use social media in our organization is pretty informal, and it looks like _____.

➜ We have not yet started to use social media in our organization, but if you have some suggestions, you can talk with _____.

➜ Your manager will meet with you regularly to let you know how you are tracking against your objectives and to give you feedback.

➜ Our culture is pretty formal (informal), so you will want to check out _____ and talk with _____ to get more insight.

➜ It's great to ask a lot of questions, and that will help you understand not only your role, but also the department and our organization's culture.

➜ Identify people who can help you get up to speed with your specific job tasks, those who have a broader view of your department or function, and those who have been in the organization longer or have a leadership role and can introduce you to our culture.

➜ Be patient and make sure you take the time to learn from those around you.

➜ It's normal to have highs and lows as you onboard, and it might take up to a year or so to really get integrated into the culture.

→ Listen, listen, and listen some more.

→ Go slow to go fast.

Perfect Phrases for Onboarding Experienced Hires

Many organizations will continue to onboard those employees who have been in the workforce for a while and are experienced in their particular fields. They obviously have different needs from an onboarding perspective, but it cannot be assumed that they do not have any transitioning issues to address. Experienced hires want their knowledge to be valued and recognized. They want to be able to leverage what they know and be able to build on it, adding to their skill sets and enabling them to go to the next levels. They also expect a clear plan with well-thought out expectations and measurements. They value an organization that can transfer their knowledge and experience into a new culture. Because they have "been around the block," experienced hires will want to have a say in their onboarding plan, but they also accept that they will be held accountable for its results.

→ Welcome! You are a great addition to our team!

→ Let's get together for coffee or lunch. I would like to hear more about your background and how we will be working together.

→ You have a really strong background and will fit in well here.

→ Some of the ways we see you using your strengths here are _____.

→ You were chosen for this role because _____
_____.

→ The overall direction of your function is _____,
and your role supports it like this: _____.

→ We have brought you in to make some changes, and it's important to build relationships first.

→ Some of the key people you will get to know first are

_____.

→ Your key internal customers are _____.

→ Your predecessor left because _____,
and this is the status of the role now: _____
_____.

→ We have started an onboarding plan with objectives for the next 90 days. With your input, we will finalize these and create measurements for them.

→ Here is the beginning of a list of your key stakeholders. We need to talk about how each of them will support your onboarding objectives, and there will be others whom you identify and add to the list as you attend your other networking meetings.

→ I have started a list of key stakeholders (people with whom you will meet over the next 90 days). Let's discuss how each will support your onboarding objectives.

→ Let's talk about your calendar and make sure you are comfortable with the pace and expectations.

→ Listen, listen, and listen some more!

→ I know that you are anxious to jump in and start delivering results, but we want you to really understand our culture and take the time to build strong relationships with the people with whom you will need to work on your objectives.

Note: This next phrase is best used for a new leader who has been selected when one or more of the current team members had also applied for the job. New managers can be blindsided by their new direct reports who wanted their position. It is best to share this confidential information with the new leader so that she can manage the situation proactively.

→ It is important for you to know that _____ also applied for but did not get your position. Some of the reasons that he did not get the position are _____ _____, and we have explained this to him so he understands. It is important that you build a good relationship with him. I would suggest that you start with a conversation.

→ Let's have a conversation about how relationships are important in our organization.

→ There are probably some differences that you have noticed about our organization from your previous one. What has been what you expected? What has been different from what you expected it to be? Are there gaps that are affecting your job?

→ Give priority to your manager's priorities.

→ Go slow to go fast.

Perfect Phrases for Onboarding Promotions or Internal Moves

One of the most neglected transitions is the promotion or internal move. This is particularly interesting because a promotion is usually a reward for outstanding work and great delivery of business results of an individual and his or her team. It is also often a move of a technical expert from an individual contributor or lower-level supervisory role to that of a management or leadership role. These are the roles that need the most support in their transition. They have the greatest chance for failure and often do fail. The crash-and-burn is blamed on the individual's inability to do the job or "lack of fit," not usually on the lack of support or resources from the organization or the inordinate number of inaccurate assumptions that were made by both the newly promoted manager and the organization. What's the solution? A well-planned, well-executed onboarding experience!

→ Forty percent of new leaders fail within the first 18 months on the job, and half of these are leaders who are promoted from within.

→ Only about 18% of organizations include promotions and internal transitions in their formal onboarding processes. We think it's important to include them to ensure success.

→ Transitioning from the field to the home office is sometimes more difficult than people think. We will make sure that your plan includes the right onboarding objectives to ensure your success.

→ Many assumptions are made about you when you get promoted. Let's talk about what some of those assumptions might be and strategies to address them.

→ People will forget that you are "new" in your role and expect you to know more than you do. Don't forget to ask questions and listen before making decisions and suggestions for changes.

→ Let's talk about your role. How do you define it? How does your manager define it? What are the gaps?

→ You might want to take advantage of some of our internal (or external) learning and development opportunities. Here is where you can find some additional resources to decide what works best for you.

→ As a new manager, you will have some unique challenges. Your manager can be a valuable resource, as well as your HR partner or another trusted leader in the organization, to guide you in the leadership style and culture of our company.

→ Getting good feedback will be another important component of your onboarding experience. We have a structured process that looks like this: _____.

→ Other ways that you can get up to speed quickly are by observing others in meetings and daily interactions, asking questions, and soliciting feedback about your behaviors and your work outputs from people you trust.

→ The relationships that you had in your former role are different from the ones you will have in your new role. There will be new people to get to know, and there will be some people that you will need to create a different type of relationship with.

→ Some of your former peers are now your direct reports. This will require a shift in thinking and beginning a new type of relationship.

→ There are new expectations for this role, and it is critical that you understand what they are and how they will be measured.

→ What are your key two or three deliverables in the first 90 days? How will these deliverables be measured?

→ You may have experienced the culture "from a distance" or from a different perspective, and people may still assume that you understand it. Do not assume that you do, and do not let others assume that you understand it.

Perfect Phrases for Onboarding Rising Stars

The high-potential employees in your organization will also be a part of at least one of the other groups that have been identified and described, for example a Gen Xer, new leader, external hire, or internal promotion. So it is important to note that a blending of approaches based on the individual needs of that particular employee is the most effective. There are some aspects of onboarding that can be highlighted to those employees who have been identified early as high potentials and who the organization wants to make sure are retained and groomed for future key leadership roles.

→ We are committed to your career development, and your onboarding plan is the first piece. We will start with your onboarding plan and work with you to implement it.

→ We understand where you've been and where you want to go, so we have drafted your onboarding plan to reflect and support both.

→ It is really important to identify people who can help you get up to speed with your specific job tasks, and also those who have a broader view of your department or function and those who have been in the organization longer or have a leadership role and can introduce you to our culture.

→ Be patient and make sure you take the time to learn from those around you.

→ The reason we hired you for this role is _____
_____.

→ The short-term plan (define "short-term," if possible) for you in this role is _____, and we will continue to develop the long-term one. I am always interested in your thoughts about how you want to grow and contribute to the organization.

For Employees Who Know They Have Been Identified as "High Potential"

→ Be committed to this role and this function—don't give the impression that this is just "another stop along the way" on your career path.

→ Quickly build relationships with your manager and peers so that you are ready if and when the next move becomes available and they support you.

→ Take advantage of every learning opportunity.

→ Do not take relationships for granted.

→ Be patient.

The workplace has become a complex mix of people from different generations, cultures, and educational, socioeconomic, and experience backgrounds. We are challenged with integrating these diverse employees into our organizations seamlessly and for the ultimate success and profitability of the organization—no small task! However, by leveraging the onboarding process and doing a few simple things consistently well, HR partners and managers can have great results with highly engaged new employees at the 100-day mark.

CHAPTER 12

Perfect Phrases for Branding Your Onboarding Experience

According to an Aberdeen Study, approximately 77 percent of U.S. companies say that they have some type of onboarding program or process in place. As with any business process, some organizations have worked to improve their onboarding programs over time and are being recognized as best-practice examples. Fifteen years ago, a candidate in the selection process of a Fortune 500 company would probably not have asked what the process was to get her integrated into the culture, her role, and the organization. Today more candidates are asking that question because of the organizations that have made onboarding part of their culture and how they do business.

Perfect Phrases for Branding Onboarding Within an Organization

Use these Perfect Phrases to brand your organization's onboarding experience into a powerful tool that will use the best of what your current market strategy has to offer:

→ Start with what you have—uncover and document your company's story, its history, its personality, its leaders, and its customers.

→ Create a "life cycle" of your product or service and make a PowerPoint, video clip, or audio download that can be posted on your website for new employees or potential employees to view or listen to.

→ Give life to concepts by telling a story of something that has meaning for your business. We have a retail client who uses the story of the "Red Blouse" that helps new employees understand how the red blouse comes to be from concept to customer, and it really works.

→ There's nothing like doing it in person. Tours, visits, days in the store, the plant, the job site, wherever and whenever you can get your new employees as close to the "action" as possible they will be engaged and be ambassadors of your brand.

→ Peak times are the best times—holidays in retail, busy season, high demand, whatever your industry defines as its peak is a great time to expose your new employees to your brand and culture. They will see it at its best, and its weaknesses will sometimes be revealed.

→ Use a "Day in the Life" experience to extend the brand to your new hires. Some organizations have their new employees participate in the customer experience so that they see firsthand what products or services are delivered. For example, in health care be the patient, in retail be the customer, in manufacturing receive and use the end product.

→ Leverage your employment brand if you have one. Spend time on the value proposition of your organization as an employer. Build the messaging of the brand into your onboarding communications through your website, e-mails, phone conversations, and orientation content.

→ Use your leaders as your brand ambassadors. It is common to have the head of finance review the budget process, but what about using her to tell about how she got integrated into the organization? Other senior leaders will be honored to be asked to participate in a new employee lunch or other event where they can tell their story or the company's story.

→ Link the oldest with the newest. I once worked for a health-care organization that valued its long-term employees and culture so much that it wanted to instill those values into the new employees. They carefully partnered some of the 20-, 30-, and 40-year employees with the orientation classes for a period of time as their onboarding buddies. This was a powerful way to teach the culture, build relationships, and get two-way feedback about how the onboarding process was working and what kept tenured employees highly engaged.

Perfect Phrases to Use While Integrating Technology into Your Onboarding Process

The use of technology with orientation and onboarding is growing. More and more technology-based solutions are becoming available in the marketplace, and they vary greatly. Many of these solutions are focused on the "paperwork" of orientation and onboarding by processing the forms needed to get a new employee into the systems and databases of an organization. This is important work and efficient, but it doesn't get the new hire acclimated or integrated into her role or the organization.

→ Create a Web-based and branded "landing page" for all new employees that gives them information on what to expect their first day or first week on the job. This page could build from the Careers/Jobs page on company website.

→ E-mail new employees after the job offer is accepted to stay in touch and send updates, company information, links, etc.

→ Use social media (LinkedIn, Facebook, Twitter, and mobile device apps) to connect and send messages to new employees during prestart.

→ Leverage your organization's intranet to create a new employee or onboarding portal to centralize access to information that is important to them during the first 90 days.

→ Create a library of onboarding resources (talking points, meeting agendas, articles, etc.) for HR partners and hiring managers to use as they coach their new employees through the onboarding process.

→ Share onboarding plans via the intranet so that hiring managers or HR partners can share best practices (and don't have to reinvent the wheel!)

→ Create Web-based "road maps" for HR partners and hiring managers to follow as they onboard their new hires.

→ Post onboarding plans on your intranet for new employees to manage.

Onboarding Success Stories from Top Companies

Branding your organization for your new employees is as important as it is for your customers. Many organizations are using their employment brand and their onboarding experience to do so. Here are a few examples of organizations that have leveraged their onboarding program into a branded competitive advantage.

Sun Microsystems

Sun Microsystems has created a unique way to engage its new hires and get them up to speed quickly. Since the company hires primarily new college graduates and younger professionals, company leaders knew that they had to create an onboarding experience that was current and engaging. They also knew that technology would play a central role in their program. So the Learning Services Design and Development group, together with the Education Leader, designed and built a video game that facilitated their onboarding process. This game is interactive and fun. It allows new employees to learn at their own pace and keeps them on track with checkpoints and reminders for due dates. It leverages the fact that most of these new employees have grown up playing video games and are comfortable with and interested in this type of learning platform.

The Ritz-Carlton Hotel Company

The Ritz-Carlton's onboarding experience is all about the company's culture of outstanding customer service. Throughout the recruitment, the job offer, and the orientation, new employees are treated as well as, or even better than, the guests of this famous hotel. They enjoy a group onboarding experience during which they hear from many of the company's top executives, learn more about the organization and its philosophies from a world-class training program, and are told that they are among the elite to have been selected as Ritz-Carlton employees. No matter what the particular role, each employee is shown how his or her contribution to the experience of clients is critical to the company's success and legacy of service.

IBM

This technology giant, which has reinvented itself over the last several years, has solved the challenge of onboarding a global workforce. Because IBM has thousands of employees dispersed in practically every country in the world, it had to create a consistent, scalable solution for onboarding new hires. IBM has built a solution using a virtual world called *Second Life*. It started as an Internet game where participants create an "avatar" or virtual representation of themselves in an online world and interact with others and their environments. IBM's leaders saw this as an opportunity to allow new hires from all parts of the globe to gather, learn, and interact in this virtual world without ever getting on a plane. They created onboarding meetings and facilitated training and question-and-answer sessions for all the participants, who not only got to know IBM, but also other new "IBM-ers" who were joining the company with them. This type of onboarding solution delivered information and also helped build relationships among people who may have never been able to meet face-to-face.

Bank of America

Bank of America has been extremely successful in its efforts to onboard its new and newly promoted leaders in the top three levels of the organization. The company's leadership development team has created a structured, yet customized program that transitions its new bank executives into their new roles. The team has created a robust program that defines what it means to be a leader at B of A and how that definition translates into the daily operations. The program focuses on helping "managers of managers" with development classes, coaching, and resources, specifically during their first 90 days. It also makes use of peer coaches and provides a team integration process for each new leader. This is a powerful process that puts the questions and issues of the team "front and center" for the leaders and gives them a structure in which to address those issues. The leadership development team's results have come from the ability of its developed leaders to take on expanded roles successfully.

Whirlpool Corporation

One of the most important features of the Whirlpool Corporation's onboarding process is how it immerses all of its new employees into the company vision, mission, and values. The company has a strong employment brand that is an extension of its product and customer service branding. The onboarding program introduces this employment brand in its deep orientation and continues to apply it as the employees move into their work areas and new roles. The onboarding process is supported by a strong commitment of the hiring managers to the idea that new employees require a chance to learn, build relationships, and start to "gain traction" in their roles by experiencing early success.

The Gap

This retail powerhouse has been onboarding long before the term became a popular buzzword in the human resources and business communities. Because of the fast pace and seasonal nature of retail, new employees could easily get overwhelmed and burned out quickly. This was especially true for new leaders who were hired for their past successes and had to "hit the ground running" in a highly competitive and not very forgiving environment. The Gap developed a process for its new and newly promoted leaders that allowed them the time to "learn and do." Company leaders emphasize the importance of establishing clearly identified onboarding objectives and building relationships across functions. The company's onboarding process encourages new leaders to learn from their managers, peers, and team while utilizing and sharing their own technical knowledge. It supports and promotes the building of those key relationships that are critical to projects and initiatives.

Clearly, with the success of onboarding in top-tier organizations, the research that supports the business case, and the unique needs of each organization and its culture, onboarding is here to stay. As with any business process, onboarding can be planned and implemented expertly with tremendous success, or it can be poorly planned, not supported, and badly executed. Some key (easy and cheap!) ways to make sure that this doesn't happen in your organization are summarized in Chapter 13.

Six Steps to Building an Effective Onboarding Experience

To quickly review, building a successful onboarding process is clearly the way to ensure that all your new employees are effectively integrated into your organization and highly engaged so that they will stay, be productive in their roles, and grow in the organization. The building of this process does not have to be overwhelming and complicated, but it must be purposeful and done within the context of your business needs. We have created a no-fail way to design and deliver the onboarding experience to best suit your unique company and its culture. Following is our recipe for how to create an onboarding process in your organization that will be sustainable and deliver the results you require.

Step 1: Define and Document Your Program's Objectives

■ We discussed establishing onboarding objectives in Chapter 1 and can't stress its importance enough. What business need(s) are you addressing with onboarding? For example, possible objectives might address speed to performance, retention, engagement, or adaption to culture.

■ Get buy-in from your leadership team and others who will be important in the rollout of the initiative.

Step 2: Identify Your Audience(s)

■ All employees is the most popular audience, but don't get stuck in a "one-size-fits-all" mentality or you won't meet your business objectives.

■ Think about leaders, internal promotions, contractors, etc. and how each group needs something slightly different.

Step 3: Capture Your Culture

■ Everyone wants to talk about how it should be, not how it is; don't make this mistake—talk about reality so there are no disconnects.

■ Put your company culture in writing and make it part of the onboarding process itself.

Step 4: Define Roles and Responsibilities

■ The new employee, the hiring manager, and the HR partner all have specific roles, and they can all be different depending on the organization.

- Who "drives" the process, and who "owns" the process?
- Get clear on roles and responsibilities before you start deciding on the actual action items, or you will have to come back to this step, and by that time you will probably have lost the trust of many of your participants.

Step 5: Build Road Maps

- Only after you have completed Steps 1 through 4 are you ready to create the "what" or the action items for each role and each time period.
- Determine what needs to be done by whom in each onboarding phase: prestart, week 1, month 1, month 2, month 3, and wrap-up.

Step 6: Measure Results

- Refer to Step 1—what business need(s) are you addressing? What data do you need to collect to see if you are addressing it or them?
- Who collects data and how?
- Build data collection (surveys and conversations) into your road maps.
- Report on both individual progress and the onboarding process, documenting trends by department, business unit, and organization.

Taking the time to work through each of these steps as you create or revamp your onboarding experience will pay off because too often organizations try to jump ahead and build the tactical parts of the program without the foundational pieces. This almost always results in poor implementation and rework. A few focused hours of time spent on Steps 1 through 5 will set you up for success as you build the rest of the onboarding experience from this foundation. We are confident that your organization will benefit as many already have from this strategic yet practical approach.

References

Martin, Kevin, and Mollie Lombardi. *Fully Onboarding: Getting the Most from Your Talent the First Year.* The Aberdeen Group, January 2009.

Sessa, Kaiser, Taylor, and Campbell. *Executive Selection: A Research Report on What Works and What Doesn't.* Center for Creative Leadership Report, 1998.

Watkins, Michael. *The First 90 Days.* Harvard Business School Press, 2003.

About the Authors

Brenda Hampel and **Erika Lamont** have consulted, coached, inspired, and developed operational and human resources teams to create onboarding and leadership development experiences at TJX Companies, Cardinal Health, Audi of America, Volkswagen Group of America, Chico's FAS, Sara Lee Food and Beverage, the Ohio State University Medical Center, Coach Inc., DSW, Victoria's Secret Stores, and NCR/Teradata. They are equally passionate about their work and their clients who drive and inspire the work.

Brenda and Erika are contributing authors to *Creating Effective Onboarding Programs* by Doris S. Sims (McGraw-Hill, 2010). They are also quoted by leadership onboarding experts in the following articles: "Obama's Onboarding Offers Lessons," SHRM online, February 2009; "Diving In" by Susan Wells, *Society for Human Resource Magazine*, 2005; "Execs on Board" by Ed Silverman, *Human Resource Executive*, 2003.

Brenda Hampel is a founding partner of Connect the Dots Consulting, LLC. She works with executive teams, functional groups, and team leaders to help them understand how to leverage their individual and combined strengths to create strategies for addressing gaps and achieving business objectives. In addition to her consulting experience with executives in Fortune 50 companies, Brenda has held human resources leadership roles at ABB; Bath & Body Works, a division of Limited Brands; and Cardinal Health.

Brenda graduated from Ohio State University with a B.A. in Communications and has continued her education by participating in executive programs (human resources curriculum) at the University of Michigan and Ohio State University.

Brenda has been invited to present at numerous professional conferences including SHRM HR Southwest Conference, the HR Technology Show, IQPC's Onboarding Talent, and CAI—HR Managers' Conference.

Erika Lamont is also a partner at Connect the Dots Consulting, LLC, and has worked with clients to create solutions for leadership onboarding, individual leadership coaching, and alignment for mergers and acquisitions, as well as team and individual skills assessment and action planning. Erika has also held various operational leadership roles inside large organizations such as Riverside Methodist Hospital, part of the OhioHealth Corporation; and Bath & Body Works, a division of Limited Brands.

Erika brings a distinctive blend of operational experience and leadership development skills to her client base. She earned a Bachelor of Arts degree in Political Science from Miami University in Oxford, Ohio, and has received extensive professional development in leadership coaching, managing teams, total quality management, supply chain development, and project management.

She has presented for national conferences in human resources such as SHRM HR Southwest, HR Tech, and IQPC Onboarding, as well as hospital association conferences and professional procurement organizations.

Both Brenda Hampel and Erika Lamont would be pleased to present workshops, speeches, and presentations on onboarding for your organization. They also provide workshops, conference sessions, speeches, presentations, and consulting in the areas of team dynamics, leadership development, and coaching.

Please contact them directly at 1-877-793-8805, bhampel @connectthedotsconsulting.com, or elamont@connectthedots consulting.com, and please visit their website and blog at www .connectthedotsconsulting.com to read the latest information about onboarding and other talent management topics.

The Right Phrase for Every Situation...Every Time

Perfect Phrases for Building Strong Teams
Perfect Phrases for Business Letters
Perfect Phrases for Business Proposals and Business Plans
Perfect Phrases for Business School Acceptance
Perfect Phrases for College Application Essays
Perfect Phrases for Cover Letters
Perfect Phrases for Customer Service
Perfect Phrases for Dealing with Difficult People
Perfect Phrases for Dealing with Difficult Situations at Work
Perfect Phrases for Documenting Employee Performance Problems
Perfect Phrases for Executive Presentations
Perfect Phrases for Landlords and Property Managers
Perfect Phrases for Law School Acceptance
Perfect Phrases for Lead Generation
Perfect Phrases for Managers and Supervisors
Perfect Phrases for Managing Your Small Business
Perfect Phrases for Medical School Acceptance
Perfect Phrases for Meetings
Perfect Phrases for Motivating and Rewarding Employees
Perfect Phrases for Negotiating Salary & Job Offers
Perfect Phrases for Perfect Hiring
Perfect Phrases for the Perfect Interview
Perfect Phrases for Performance Reviews
Perfect Phrases for Real Estate Agents & Brokers
Perfect Phrases for Resumes
Perfect Phrases for Sales and Marketing Copy
Perfect Phrases for the Sales Call
Perfect Phrases for Sales Presentations
Perfect Phrases for Setting Performance Goals
Perfect Phrases for Small Business Owners
Perfect Phrases for the TOEFL Speaking and Writing Sections
Perfect Phrases for Writing Company Announcements
Perfect Phrases for Writing Grant Proposals
Perfect Phrases in American Sign Language for Beginners
Perfect Phrases in French for Confident Travel
Perfect Phrases in German for Confident Travel
Perfect Phrases in Italian for Confident Travel
Perfect Phrases in Spanish for Confident Travel to Mexico
Perfect Phrases in Spanish for Construction
Perfect Phrases in Spanish for Gardening and Landscaping

Visit mhprofessional.com/perfectphrases for a complete product listing.

Learn more. Do more.

CPSIA information can be obtained
at www.ICGtesting.com
Printed in the USA
FFOW04n0143281115
18903FF